# Hostile Sea

## The U-Boat Offensive around the Isle of Man during World War One

**Adrian Corkill**

**Above:** a U-Boat deck gun and crew. (Courtesy of CriticalPast)

# Acknowledgements

The author would like to thank the following people and organisations in particular for their invaluable help in writing this book:

Chris Michael, Deirdre Murray for permission to reproduce the photograph of her grandfather
The UK National Archives , Manx National Heritage, The National Maritime Museum
The Imperial War Museum, The World Ship Society

A special thank you to my partner Allison Fox for her valuable advice and help with checking the text.

# Copyright Notice

Cover design and typesetting by Jacob Beard, Mannin Digital & Design
Cover images courtesy of CriticalPast
First published 2013
Copyright © 2013 Adrian Corkill – First Edition
ISBN: 978-0-9540115-2-9
Printed by Mannin Printing, Media House, Cronkbourne, Douglas, Isle of Man

This book is dedicated to all who lost their lives in the seas around the Isle of Man during World War One.

# Contents

# Guide to the information box

| | |
|---|---|
| **Location** | |
| 53 55.341 N | Latitude where the event took place |
| 04 55.264 W | Longitude where the event took place |
| | |
| 10 miles southwest by west of the Calf of Man | Description of where the event took place according to historical sources (distances in nautical miles) |
| **Vessel** | |
| Steel steamship | Construction material and type of vessel |
| London | Port of registration |
| ON 99,099 | Official number |
| 2,583 tons gross, 1,617 tons net | Gross and net tonnage |
| 1892 by J Blumer and Company, Sunderland | Year built and shipyard details |
| Triple-expansion engine, 249 nhp, North East Marine Engineering Limited, Sunderland | Engine type, horse power and engine maker |
| Page Shipping Company Limited (John I Jacobs and Company Limited, London, manager) – on charter to the British Government | Owner's details (manager's details) |
| 305.9 ft x 41.1 ft x 18.8 ft | Dimensions in feet |
| 93.3 m x 12.5 m x 5.7 m | Dimensions in metres |
| Ex Clan Macrae | Previous name(s) |
| Ex Shatt-El-Arab | |

Where the longitude and latitude co-ordinates of a wreck site are given they have been obtained using the datum WGS84 and GPS units should be adjusted to use this datum.

# Introduction

Many of us are familiar with the Battle of the Atlantic in World War Two when Nazi Germany's U-Boats wrought havoc with Allied convoys bringing supplies to Great Britain from North America in the vast expanse of the Atlantic Ocean. Few members of the Manx public are, however, aware of the German U-boat offensive closer to home during World War One. German U-Boats patrolled in the seas around the Isle of Man seeking ships to destroy and sending many a steamship to the bottom by use of deck gun, torpedo, bomb or mine. Allied warships guarded convoys and conducted anti-submarine operations whenever they could. After the initial offensive by U-Boats in the Irish Sea in the first few months of 1915 the British press was censored. Any news of losses or damage to shipping was omitted from newspapers, including those published in the Isle of Man, in an attempt to disguise the real extent of the effectiveness of the German naval blockade, a military strategy designed to starve Great Britain into submission. Therefore, little recollection of the events of World War One in the seas around the Isle of Man exists in the collective memory of the Manx nation and this is the first time that many of the events in this book have been made available to the public.

In researching this book I have concentrated my efforts in the British records and in particular those of the British Admiralty which consist of witness reports and the official report on each event. There is always the danger when using the records from one side in a conflict that a biased interpretation of events will result but where possible I have corroborated facts with those from other sources. Researching the U-Boat archives in Germany was discounted due to the language barrier together with the considerable time and cost that would have been involved in such a task. Accepting the limitations to the research it is my expectation that this book will be of great value, not only to the Manx public, but to military and family historians all over the world.

The Imperial German Navy commissioned its first U-Boat, *U-1,* on 14th December 1906. In only 8 years, German submarine technology had developed by leaps and bounds, to the extent that by the start of World War One in August 1914, U-Boats could operate hundreds of miles from their bases in Germany. They were soon conducting patrols into the Irish Sea as early as January 1915. Despite this, U-Boats in World War One could best be described as boats that *"occasionally dived underwater"* in order to avoid enemy detection. Most of the time they effectively operated as surface ships. This made them vulnerable to Allied attack but it took the Allies until 1917 to develop the hardware, tactics and technology to really make an impact on U-Boat numbers. By the end of the war the U-Boat threat had been effectively neutralised. However, no U-Boats were lost in the waters around the Isle of Man during World War One, with the possible exception of *U-69* which may have gone missing in the Irish Sea after 24th July 1917.

The destruction wrought by U-Boats was out of all proportion to their numbers and in all around 420 people lost their lives in the events described in this book. This figure may surprise many readers as it is not generally considered that the war caused so many casualties so close to home. A broad range of vessel types were attacked or sunk by U-Boats or destroyed by the mines they laid around the Manx coast, including military ships, cargo steamers, passenger ferries and fishing vessels. It is interesting to note that no U-Boat ever made an attack on an Isle of Man Steam Packet Company vessel despite the ships posing an obvious and easy target for the U-Boats. Neither did they lay mines on routes used by the Isle of Man Steam Packet Company boats. The reason behind this lay with the presence of numerous internment and prisoner of war camps on the Isle of Man containing thousands of German nationals. U-Boat commanders were briefed not to attack Isle of Man Steam Packet Company ships, which were used to ferry their fellow countrymen to and from the Isle of Man.

The events include attacks on ships, the sinking of ships, operations against U-Boats by Allied defences and events that occurred elsewhere outside Manx waters but had a direct connection with the Isle of Man, such as bodies washed ashore on the Manx coast. The book is split into five periods of U-Boat activity. Surprisingly there were long periods of little or no U-Boat activity around the Isle of Man. The book also contains a list of all those who were known to have been lost in the activity. Where known, a short description of the wreck site is given, together with the GPS coordinates.

There is only one photograph known to exist of the U-Boat offensive around the Isle of Man – *HMS Champagne* breaking in two after being torpedoed off the west coast of the Isle of Man – so it is difficult to illustrate the book with photographs of the events covered. Nevertheless, I hope the unique content and informative nature of this book will make it a valued and much thumbed addition to your book collection.

Adrian Corkill, May 2013

# The Early Engagements

The British Admiralty commenced the naval blockade of Germany in August 1914 soon after Britain had declared war on Germany on 4th August. In early November 1914 the British declared the entire North Sea to be a War Zone. The Germans considered this move to be a blatant attempt to starve the German people into submission and sought retaliation in kind.

Germany could not match Britain in terms of the naval strength of its surface fleet and its only possible way to blockade the seas around the British Isles was by using U-Boats. On 4th February 1915 Admiral Hugo von Pohl responded to the British declaration of war by publishing a warning in the Imperial German Gazette (Deutscher Reichsanzeiger):

*"All the waters surrounding Great Britain and Ireland, including the whole of the English Channel, are hereby declared to be a War Zone. From February 18 onwards every enemy merchant vessel found within this War Zone will be destroyed without it always being possible to avoid danger to the crews and passengers.*

*Neutral ships will also be exposed to danger in the War Zone, as, in view of the misuse of neutral flags ordered on January 31 by the British Government, and owing to unforeseen incidents to which naval warfare is liable, it is impossible to avoid attacks being made on neutral ships in mistake for those of the enemy.*

*Navigation to the north of the Shetlands, in the eastern parts of the North Sea and through a zone at least thirty nautical miles wide along the Dutch coast is not exposed to danger."*

Thus began the first wave of unrestricted submarine warfare.

But events in the Irish Sea began a few days before this declaration. On Friday 29th January 1915 at about 1.50 pm a submarine was observed at a range of 9,500 yards steaming slowly towards land in shallow water due west of Fort Walney gun battery on Walney Island near Barrow-in-Furness, manned by Number 7 Company of the Lancashire and Cheshire R.G.A. The battery commander instantly telephoned to the Port War Signal Station and to Messrs Vickers, the submarine makers in Barrow-in-Furness, and was informed that nothing was known about the possible presence of a friendly boat off Walney Island. The guns were manned and readied.

All appearances pointed to the submarine being German and belonging to the *"U"* class. Her nationality was soon declared when at 2.25 pm one shot was fired by her in the direction of a recently completed airship shed at a range of 7,200 yards. This round fell approximately 1,000 yards short.

The battery opened fire. The submarine fired two more rounds, the last falling in line with the battery about 100 yards from the shore. Eleven rounds of lyddite shell in all were fired by the battery. The battery commander stated that the target was not an easy one for the gun layers and that the smoke took sometime to clear. Therefore, the rate of fire was slow. Two changes of deflection on the guns were made necessary by the course of the submarine, which first approached the battery from the northwest and then turned sharply to the north. She disappeared at a range of 6,900 yards; the battery had been in action for just 3 minutes. The submarine was the *U-21,* commanded by Kapitänleutnant Otto Hersing and was the first of many German submarines to enter the Irish Sea to attack enemy shipping and land targets.

There was some reason to believe that the *U-21* was on reconnaissance near Walney Island, with a view to locating any fixed defences. It is moreover possible that a further attack on the airship shed or shipyard may have been considered.

The following day Hersing attacked and sunk three ships off Liverpool Bay, including the steamship *Kilcoan*. Hersing was awarded the Iron Cross on his return to Germany.

The steamship *Downshire* was sunk off the Calf of Man on 20th February 1915 by *U-30*. This was the only casualty in the vicinity of the Isle of Man during the early engagements although the *Princess Victoria* was sunk nearby in March 1915 and bodies from the sinking of the steamship *Bayano* were washed ashore on the Isle of Man.

The early forays by U-Boats into the Irish Sea in the first quarter of 1915 were clearly a demonstration by the German Navy that they could take their blockade right to the very centre of British waters. In reality the operational capabilities of the early U-Boats did not match German aspirations.

There were no further casualties from U-Boat attacks around the Isle of Man until the latter part of 1916.

**Location**
53 40.230 N
03 41.190 W

18 miles northwest of the
Liverpool Bar Lightship

**Vessel**
Steel steamship
Belfast
ON 120,708
422 tons gross, 162 tons net
1905 by Ailsa Steam Boat
Company Limited, Ayr
Compound steam engine, 72
rhp, Muir and Houston Limited,
Glasgow
Howden Brothers, Larne
163.0 ft x 25.0 ft x 10.0 ft
49.7 m x 7.6 m x 3.0 m

13.30 hours
30th January 1915

# Sinking of the steamship *Kilcoan*

The German submarines commenced their Irish Sea offensive against shipping on Saturday 30th January 1915, when three trading vessels were sunk. The first of these was the steamship *Ben Cruachan*, of Newcastle, a large steamer of 3,092 tons gross, proceeding from Scapa Flow after having delivered 4,000 tons of Welsh coal to the British Fleet. She was returning to Liverpool to discharge the remaining 966 tons of her cargo when at 10.30 am, some 18 miles northwest of the Liverpool Bar Lightship, she was intercepted by the German submarine *U-21*, under Kapitänleutnant Otto Hersing. Her 23 crew was given 10 minutes to leave their vessel.

They boarded and launched the two lifeboats. The Germans then exploded what appeared to be a mine alongside the *Ben Cruachan* and she commenced sinking immediately, finally plunging below the waves at 11.00 am. The Germans directed the crew of the *Ben Cruachan* to steer the lifeboats towards a trawler and they were picked up by the *Margaret* an hour later and conveyed to Fleetwood. Captain Heggie, master of the *Ben Cruachan*, failed to destroy the ship's papers and these fell into the hands of the Germans.

The second ship to succumb to the submarine offensive that day was the steamship *Linda Blanche*, of Beaumaris, under Captain John Ellis, master, which had left Manchester at 6.00 pm on Friday 29th January 1915 bound for Belfast with a general cargo weighing 200 tons. All went well until 12.20 pm on Saturday 30th January when the *U-21* surfaced about a quarter of a mile from her. The *Linda Blanche* was about 18 miles northwest ½ north from the Liverpool Bar Lightship. The *U-21* hoisted the German flag and signalled

**Above:** *SS Ben Cruachan.*

the steamer to stop. The *U-21* then pulled alongside the *Linda Blanche* and the men on the submarine handed out cigars and cigarettes to the crew of the *Linda Blanche* before giving them 10 minutes to get all their boats out and leave their ship. A German officer took all the documents relating to the ship and cargo, together with two of the charts. The *Linda Blanche* was then sunk by two bombs in the forecastle. The crew of the *Linda Blanche* were instructed to steer a course to take them to a fishing vessel.

Whilst trawling 16 miles west-southwest from Morecambe Bay Lightship at 12.30 pm the skipper of the steam trawler *Niblick* saw an explosion about 2 miles to the north coming from a steamer. The crew of the *Niblick* saw her rear up on her keel and suddenly sink. The steam trawler at once took in her fishing gear and proceeded towards the scene. After about 15 minutes, they came into contact with a lot of wreckage, but saw no bodies. After cruising around, the *Niblick* spotted two specks to the windward. Steaming towards them, they came across the two lifeboats from the *Linda Blanche*. The *Niblick* took on board the eleven man crew of the *Linda Blanche* and steamed at full speed to land them at Fleetwood at 7.00 pm.

The third and final ship to be destroyed on this single day was the *Kilcoan,* of Belfast. The *Kilcoan,* under Captain James Meneely, master, left Garston on Saturday 30th January 1915 bound for Belfast with a cargo of 470 tons of coal and a crew of eleven men. Captain Meneely piloted his vessel down the Mersey and she reached the Liverpool Bar Lightship at 11.55 am and course then set northwest ¼ north for the Chicken Rock, off the Isle of Man. He went below for dinner leaving the mate in charge of the *Kilcoan*. He came back on deck at 12.15 pm and swapped places with the mate who went below for his dinner. When the mate arrived back on the bridge at 12.45 pm Captain Meneely went below for rest. At 1.30 pm when she was 18 miles northwest from the Liverpool Bar Lightship, a submarine flying the White Ensign came alongside. The mate shouted down to the master, *"Come on deck. Here is a submarine which wishes to speak to us"*. Captain Meneely immediately went on deck and saw the *U-21*, painted a dull white colour on the hull and bridge and a darker colour on her conning tower. A machine gun was trained on the steamer and a number of men, armed with revolvers and rifles, were stationed on the conning tower. The White Ensign was then lowered and the master and crew of the *Kilcoan* were ordered to take to their boats and to hand all the ship's papers over to the submarine.

The submarine directed the crew of the *Kilcoan* to row to the small steamship *Gladys,* of Liverpool. The *Gladys*, owned by the Monks Line, had left Garston on Saturday 30th January with a cargo of coal for the Douglas Gas Light Company and about 2.30 pm, when about 18 miles northwest of the Liverpool Bar Lightship, she was hailed by *U-21* which came alongside her. Kapitänleutnant Hersing ordered the *Gladys* to follow him to another steamer close by. Evidently he had taken the *Gladys* for a steam trawler, as she had a large *"M"* on her funnel similar to a trawler's mark, and she also had a mizzen sail up. On coming up to the *Kilcoan,* they found her crew in two boats, which the *Gladys* took in tow. The Germans afterwards boarded the *Kilcoan*, took the ship's Ensign and the Union Jack,

**Above:** *SS Linda Blanche.*

and fired an explosive charge amidships on her main deck to sink her. The *Kilcoan* slid below the waves at 3.40 pm. Kapitänleutnant Hersing then ordered the *Gladys* to convey the *Kilcoan's* crew to Douglas rather than return to Liverpool, as no doubt Hersing was anxious that his presence in the vicinity be kept secret as long as possible. The *Gladys* arrived in Douglas harbour at 10.00 pm and the crew of the *Kilcoan* were landed and helped by the Douglas harbour master, Captain George E Kelly, who as agent for the Shipwrecked Mariners Association, found them lodgings for the night.

## Wreck Site
Latitude 53 40.230 N, Longitude 03 41.190 W

The probable wreck of the *Kilcoan* lies in 35 metres of water on a muddy seabed. The length of wreck is 50 metres, width 10 metres and height 8 metres. It is orientated 135/315 degrees. The steamship lies on its starboard side with the bow facing northwest. The wreck is broken up from the bow to the boiler, but the stern section is fairly intact.

## Paper Sources
British Vessels Lost at Sea 1914-1918 and 1939-1945, HMSO
Chris Michael
Lloyd's Wars Losses, the First World War, Casualties to Shipping through Enemy Causes 1914-1918
Mona's Herald Thursday 03.02.1915. Manx National Heritage
Ramsey Courier Friday 05.02.1915. Manx National Heritage
The National Archives of the UK (TNA): Public Record Office (PRO) ADM137/1047, ADM137/1057 and ADM137/2959

**Location**
54 00.115 N
05 01.655 W

9 miles west of the Calf of Man

**Vessel**
Steel steamship
Belfast
ON 108,621
337 tons gross, 126 tons net
1898 by Ailsa Shipbuilding
Company, Troon
Compound steam engine, 65
rhp, Muir and Houston Limited,
Glasgow
East Downshire Steamship
Company Limited, Dundrum
156.9 ft x 24.1 ft x 9.1 ft
47.8 m x 7.3 m x 2.8 m

18.00 hours
20th February 1915

# Sinking of the steamship *Downshire*

The *Downshire*, under Captain William Henry Connor, master, left Dundrum at 2.00 pm on Saturday 20th February 1915 for Ellesmere Port, after having discharged a cargo of Whitehaven coal. The vessel was practically light, having only about 100 bundles of cement sacks as cargo and was due to load with coal and sundries for her home port. At 6.00 pm she was about 9 miles west of the Calf of Man when the watch on deck spotted a submarine about 2 miles away, on her starboard bow, coming from a southerly direction. Captain Connor immediately gave orders for the vessel to be turned onto a northerly course, to proceed at full steam and to make smoke. The usual speed of the *Downshire* was about 8 to 9 knots but was making 10 in her endeavours to get away from the submarine. This, however, was impossible as the submarine was doing 15 to 16 knots. When within close range the U-Boat fired a shot across the bows of the *Downshire* quickly followed by two others. When the third shot was fired the *Downshire* reluctantly stopped and hauled down the Ensign, the crew waiting on deck for further developments. The submarine was now within fifty yards when one of the officers hailed, in perfect English, *"Put out your boats and get into them"*. During this operation the submarine had its deck gun trained on the crew of the *Downshire.*

Suddenly the exhaust steam began to blow out and the *Downshire's* crew were ordered to stop it, the commander of the submarine being evidently suspicious lest they should try to escape. The chief engineer went down and pumped out the boiler and the noise stopped. The two engineers and three of the sailors got into one of the lifeboats, and the Captain, the first and second mates, two firemen and the cook got into the second. This boat was ordered to row to the submarine, which was about 50 yards away from the steamer. The occupants were directed on board the submarine and the German officer said to Captain Connor, *"We are sorry to sink the ship but the British were attempting to starve out Germany."* The other lifeboat was meanwhile ordered to row away in a westerly direction. The German skipper put five of his sailors into the lifeboat, and he ordered two of the *Downshire's* crew to row the lifeboat back to the ship. They took a bomb with them, a round brass canister, about 4 inches by 8 inches, and they passed a rope round the bottom of the ship with the bomb attached. Meanwhile, the Germans advised the cook to get any necessary provisions and to take them with him into the lifeboat. The Germans conducted a quick search of the vessel taking the ship's papers with them before touching a time fuse. They all reboarded the lifeboat and rowed back to the submarine. Shortly afterwards, a faint noise from the explosion was heard, and slowly the steamer settled down taking a slight list to port. When the water was almost level with the deck, the steamer descended into the sea head foremost.

The first officer of the *Downshire,* Manxman Thomas Turnbull, asked the German officer why they had sunk the *Downshire* when there were numerous trawlers and fishing boats in the area. The German replied that they had orders to sink only trading vessels. The crew of the *Downshire* were then told to row away before the submarine, *U-30,* under Korvettenkapitän Erich von Rosenberg-Gruszczyski, disappeared. Shortly afterwards, they spotted two trawlers and hailed them. As most of the crew were from Dundrum, the Lowestoft trawlers *Kipper* and *Golden News* landed them at Dundrum at about midnight.

The crew of the *Downshire* was:

CARDSWELL, James, fireman, Dundrum
CARLYLE, Thomas, fireman, Dundrum
CONNOR, John, second officer, Dundrum
CONNOR, William Henry, master, Belfast
ERICKSON, James, second engineer, Belfast
McGOWAN, William, seaman, Dundrum
MARTIN, William, steward, Dundrum
MORRISON, Alex, seaman, Dundrum
MULLAN, John, chief engineer, Dundrum
MURPHY, Henry, seaman, Dundrum
TURNBULL, Thomas, chief officer, Croit-e-Caley, Isle of Man

In a letter from the Admiralty dated 2nd March 1915 it was stated, *"The vessel was 15 miles from Peel in deep water. She was in a favourable position for ramming the submarine, but being such a small vessel and not having received any advice on the subject, it is doubtful whether she could reasonably be expected to do so, some skippers would probably have risked the attempt. Her shallow draught would have saved her from being torpedoed in the event of missing, and she might have thus escaped."*

**Wreck Site**

Latitude 54 00.115 N, Longitude 05 01.655 W

The probable wreck of the *Downshire* lies in 65 metres of water on a muddy seabed several miles south of the official position of her loss of 8 miles northwest ½ west from the Calf of Man but in a position that would be expected from her voyage from Dundrum to the entrance of the Mersey. The length of wreck is 50 metres, width 10 metres and height 5 metres. It is orientated 110/290 degrees. The wreck shows no evidence of cargo in the two cargo holds which lie between the bow and bridge of the vessel. The wreck sits on its keel and is fairly intact but most of the superstructure has perished away.

**Paper Sources**

British Vessels Lost at Sea 1914-1918 and 1939-1945, HMSO

Isle of Man Examiner Saturday 27.02.1915. Manx National Heritage

Isle of Man Times Saturday 27.02.1915. Manx National Heritage

Lloyd's Register 1915

Lloyd's Wars Losses, the First World War, Casualties to Shipping through Enemy Causes 1914-1918

Mona's Herald Wednesday 24.02.1915. Manx National Heritage

The National Archives of the UK (TNA): Public Record Office (PRO) ADM137/1057

World Ship Society

**Location**
53 37.930 N
03 39.340 W

16 miles northwest by north of
the Liverpool Bar Lightship

**Vessel**
Steel steamship
Glasgow
ON 102,665
1,095 tons gross, 432 tons net
1894 by W B Thompson and
Company, Dundee
Triple-expansion engine, 201
nhp, W B Thompson and
Company, of Dundee
M Langlands and Sons, 45 Hope
Street, Glasgow
245.0 ft x 35.1 ft x 15.2 ft
74.7 m x 10.7 m x 4.6 m

09.10 hours
9th March 1915

# Sinking of the steamship

## *Princess Victoria*

The *Princess Victoria,* under Captain John Cubbin, master, left Aberdeen at 4.00 pm on Saturday 6th March 1915 bound for Liverpool with 1,100 tons of general cargo and a crew of 24 men.

The *Princess Victoria* often passed through Ramsey Bay. She had accommodation for about 200 passengers, and during the summer season was utilised for trips around Scotland and for tourist visits to some of the remote islands west of Scotland. In the winter she was used for transporting cargo only.

All went well until 4.00 am on Tuesday 9th March when she passed Maughold Head on the northeast coast of the Isle of Man. The weather was gloriously fine, with no wind and the sea like glass.

Little did Captain Cubbin know, but his ship was being targeted by *U-20*, under Kapitänleutnant Walther Schwieger, commander. This was the very submarine which, a few months later, torpedoed and sank the *Lusitania* off the Old Head of Kinsale, Ireland. By 9.10 am the *Princess Victoria* had run another 45 miles on the log, when in a position 16 miles northwest by north of the Liverpool Bar Lightship and heading southeast by south, the second mate, who was on lookout duty, suddenly shouted, *"Look-out, look-out! What's this?"* Captain Cubbin looked and saw a torpedo and its wake approaching his vessel on the starboard side forward of her beam and at very high speed. Before he could issue any orders the torpedo struck the *Princess Victoria* on her starboard side almost abreast of number one hatch. The explosion smashed the bottom out of the steamer and blew the cargo up through the hatches. The column of water thrown up by the explosion smashed the lifeboat swung out on the starboard side. The vessel immediately listed over to starboard and began to sink by the head. Her crew left the stricken steamer in the two port lifeboats. The *Princess Victoria* disappeared beneath the waves at 9.30 am. The occupants of the two boats were picked up by the steam trawler *Ocean Harvest* which towed the two lifeboats to Liverpool.

Captain Cubbin was from the Isle of Man, along with a contingent of fellow Manxmen: chief officer, C Hugh Kinley, of Surby; T Hudson, of Castletown; Ed Killey, of Patrick; J Colvin, of Peel; N Killey, of Peel; C Gorry, of Peel; and W Morrison, of Douglas.

**Above:** *SS Princess Victoria.*

Chief officer Hugh Kinley had a thrilling escape. He had only been relieved from his duty a short time before, and was in his bunk asleep, when the ship was torpedoed. The impact threw him violently across the bunk, and his head struck a hard surface which temporarily stunned him. Fortunately, he quickly recovered, and his first thoughts were that they had been in collision with another vessel. On trying to open the door of the cabin he found it had jammed owing to the buckling of the ship. Putting on a pair of sea clogs, which were close by, he vigorously kicked the door open and got on deck. The vessel went down shortly afterwards.

**Wreck Site**

Latitude 53 37.930 N, Longitude 03 39.340 W

The confirmed wreck of the *Princess Victoria* lies in 35 metres of water (the bell was recovered in 1994). The length of wreck is 80 metres, width 15 metres and height 10 metres. It is orientated 000/180 degrees. The bow lists to starboard, while the mid-ships section is upright and the stern lists to port. Much of the wreck has collapsed but the engine room and superstructure are fairly intact. The stern section has also collapsed with the stern post standing proud.

**Paper Sources**

British Merchant Ships Sunk by U-Boats in the 1914-1918 War, Tennent

British Vessels Lost at Sea 1914-1918 and 1939-1945, HMSO

Isle of Man Examiner Saturday 13.03.1915. Manx National Heritage

Lloyd's Wars Losses, the First World War, Casualties to Shipping through Enemy Causes 1914-1918

Lloyd's Register 1914

Ramsey Courier Friday 12.03.1915. and 19.03.1915. Manx National Heritage

The National Archives of the UK (TNA): Public Record Office (PRO) ADM137/1057 and ADM137/2959

# HMS Bayano
# - recovery of bodies
# and inquests

An inquest was conducted by High-Bailiff Gell at the Douglas Court House on Friday morning 19th March 1915 on three of the crew of *HMS Bayano* which had been sunk the previous week by a German submarine. The bodies were found in the water 12 miles southwest by west of the Mull of Galloway on Tuesday 16th March 1915 by the steam trawler *Norse* and taken into Douglas.

The Glasgow steamer *Bayano*, 5,938 tons gross, had been an Elders and Fyffe's liner until requisitioned by the Admiralty on 21st November 1914 as an auxiliary cruiser and armed with two 6-inch guns. At 5.15 am on Thursday 11th March 1915, under the command of Captain H C Carr, she was bound from the Clyde for Liverpool to load a cargo of coal, when she was intercepted and torpedoed by the German submarine *U-27*, under Kapitänleutnant Bernd Wegener, about 10 miles northwest by west of Corsewall Point off the southwest coast of Scotland. *HMS Bayano* sank rapidly in 3 minutes taking the lives of fourteen officers including Captain Carr and 181 ratings. Only four officers and 22 ratings survived.

Coroner Gell revealed the identity of the first body as that of leading seaman James Raymond Geraghty, of St Mary Magdalene Lodge, Northwald Way, Mortlake, London. He had telegraphed to the relations, but they were unable to attend the inquiry. The second body was that of Sergeant Arthur Grey King, the Marine Light Infantry, who resided at 79 Florence Road, Southall, Middlesex and who left a widow but she was also unable to attend the inquiry. The identification of the third body awaited the arrival of a survivor of the *Bayano*, First Class Petty Officer Benjamin John Cummings, at Douglas so it was not until Saturday 20th March 1915 at the adjourned inquest that it was identified as that of First Class Petty Officer A A Hellyer (number 143,281), of Portsmouth.

**Above:** *HMS Bayano.*

All three bodies when found had lifebelts on, and the medical evidence showed that death was due to exposure rather than drowning. The bodies of Geraghty and Hellyer were interred at Douglas Borough Cemetery on Sunday 21st March 1915. Thousands of the inhabitants of the Isle of Man watched the cortege pass from the Rocket Brigade Station at the Red Pier (approximately where the Edward Pier is now) to the cemetery, and many were visibly affected by the White Ensign, placed on the hearses by members of the Coastguard and Rocket Brigade. The military made the usual evolution, and afterwards walked with arms reversed. The Isle of Man Volunteers, under Sergeant W Morgan, preceded by the Douglas Town Band, headed the procession, and following in their wake came the Rocket Brigade, under First Officer George Moore; Lieutenant Weales, Divisional Officer of the Coastguards; a section of the Loyal Manx Association, under Section Commander A E Rothwell; a detachment of the National Reserve; the Mayor of Douglas, D Flinn, and members of the Town Council, together with officials of the Corporation; and the Fire Brigade under Superintendent O'Hara.

With slow tread and to the solemn strains of the *"Dead March,"* the cortege proceeded on its way to the cemetery. Reverend H F Shenton, vicar of St Barnabas', conducted the ceremony for Hellyer and Father Coagley, curate of St Mary's, conducted the ceremony for Geraghty. After last prayers had been offered, in each case, the firing party discharged a volley over the dead men's graves, and buglers sounded the *"Last Post."* At the close of the funeral, the Reverend Shenton said, *"I voice the feelings of this great crowd when I say how desirous we all are to extend our sympathy to the sorrowing widow and daughter of this dead hero. It seems stranger that, in a little island like this, one should be called upon to fulfil an office of this kind and commit to his last resting place one who died in warfare. We in Douglas are anxious to do our utmost to honour the memory of this hero who dies as truly at the post of duty as the man who dies with his face to the foe."*

The following day the body of Petty Officer Herbert Benjamin Williams was brought into Ramsey by the Fleetwood trawler *Adventurer.*

**Above:** The graves today in Douglas Borough Cemetery.

## Paper Sources
Glasgow Herald Saturday 13.03.1915.
Isle of Man Examiner Saturday 20.03.1915. Manx National Heritage
Mona's Herald Wednesday 24.03.1915. Manx National Heritage
Ramsey Courier Friday 19.03.1915. Manx National Heritage
Wigtown Free Press Thursday 18.03.1915.

**Location**
54 08.750 N
04 28.100 W

Outer harbour, Douglas

**Vessel**
Wooden yacht
Peel
ON 67,858
12 tons gross, 10 tons net
1906 by Watterson and Neakle,
Peel
4-cylinder petrol engine, 16 hp,
Kelvin
James Bent, Mafeking, Bradda
West Road, Port Erin
40.9 ft x 12.5 ft x 5.6 ft
12.5 m x 3.8 m x 1.7 m

00.00 hours
28th August 1915

# Destruction of
# *RN Yacht Dolores*

The auxiliary cruiser *HMS Bayano* was torpedoed in the North Channel on Thursday 11th March 1915, one of her crew being brought to Ramsey, dead, and many other bodies being washed up on the coast of the Isle of Man. A patrol of the Manx coast was established about this time; the auxiliary yacht *Dolores,* under the command of Lieutenant H B Mylchreest, RNVR, with Sub-Lieutenant C C Buckler, RNVR, as second in command, being used by the Royal Navy for the purpose. Early on Sunday morning 28th August 1915, whilst lying at anchor in Douglas outer harbour, she caught fire. The flames spread with great rapidity and though those on board got the boat alongside the breakwater and the Douglas Fire Brigade were sent for, they were unable to save the boat, which had to be sunk to put out the flames.

The wreck was subsequently raised and moved to the lifeboat slipway. A quantity of salvaged equipment from the wreck was sold by auction at the Harbour Commissioners yard on Thursday 23rd September 1915, including the engine, gearbox and propeller.

**Paper Sources**
British Vessels Lost At Sea 1914-1918 and 1939-1945, HMSO
Peel Shipping Register 1864-1893 folio 52, Manx National Heritage
Ramsey Courier Friday 03.09.1915. and 01.10.1915. Manx National Heritage
The Isle of Man and the Great War, B E Sargeaunt
World Ship Society

# The Mining Offensive

From the end of March 1915 to the beginning of November 1916 there was no U-Boat activity in the seas around the Isle of Man and very little anywhere in the Irish Sea. It was a period of 19 months in which shipping could pass safely through Manx waters without fear of attack by U-Boats. Most U-Boat activity during this period was confined to the Mediterranean, the Western Approaches off southwest England and the North Sea.

After the first restricted campaign of 1915 the German Navy returned to a strategy of using its U-Boats to attempt to erode the British Grand Fleet, which was numerically superior, by staging a series of operations designed to lure the Grand Fleet into U-Boat traps. However, at this stage in the war, U-Boats were still slow compared to surface ships so these operations required U-Boat patrol lines to be set up, while the German High Seas Fleet manoeuvred to draw the British Grand Fleet to them. Operations were staged in the North Sea during March and April 1916 but with no success.

When the British Grand Fleet did finally engage with the German High Seas Fleet in the Battle of Jutland in May 1916 no U-Boats were involved in the action. A further series of operations conducted in August and October 1916 were equally unsuccessful.

Despite the tactic of using U-Boats to lure the Grand fleet into traps proving unsuccessful it did give the German Navy the impetus to design and build better U-Boats capable of mounting an effective campaign on Allied shipping.

The strangling effect of the Allied naval blockade on Germany and the continuing lack of progress by the German Army on the Western Front, especially at the Somme and Verdun, was causing concern for the German leadership and on 30th August 1916, a conference was held at Pless (in modern day Poland) at which the Chief of Naval Staff, Admiral Henning Holtzendorff, once again proposed that the U-Boat offensive against shipping should recommence. Von Jagow, the Foreign Minister, and Secretary of State Helfferich continued to oppose the proposal prophesising that, *"Germany will be treated like a mad dog"* if the U-Boats attacked world shipping. No decision was taken at the conference, but consideration was given to building 21 new U-Boats. In hindsight this number would prove totally inadequate and contributed to the eventual failure of the U-Boat offensive later in 1918.

The authority for a renewed offensive against Allied shipping was issued 2 months later in October 1916. Bearing in mind the fear of bad press for the offensive great stress was laid on the necessity of observing the formalities of international law. The safety of the target ship's crew was still paramount and the U-Boats were ordered to surface and examine intended targets before sinking them. As a final safety precaution U-Boats were advised to let ships pass if there was any doubt over the ship's neutrality. But despite the order not to attack ships without warning U-Boat captains often did exactly that.

One method to mount an attack without warning, but at the same time not risk the safety of the U-Boat and her crew during the attack, was to lay mines in enemy shipping lanes. A minefield was laid by *U-80* to the southeast of the Isle of Man off Langness at the beginning of November 1916 and was clearly an attempt to sink vessels going around the south of the Isle of Man to and from the port of Liverpool. Three steamships were lost: the *Skerries*, *Opal* and *Liverpool*; and the liner *Celtic* was damaged by a mine a few miles south of Castletown.

**Vessel**
Steel steamship
Glasgow
ON 124,137
4,278 tons gross, 2,702 tons net
1906 by Russell and Company,
Glasgow
Triple-expansion engine, 410
nhp, Rankin and Blakemore,
Greenock
Clyde Shipping Company,
Glasgow
370.4 ft x 49.8 ft x 19.1 ft
112.9 m x 15.2 m x 5.8 m

15.00 hours
4th November 1916

# Sinking of the steamship *Skerries*

At 3.00 pm on Saturday 4th November 1916 the *Skerries*, under Captain Henry R Bryden, master, bound from Barrow-in-Furness, Cumbria, for Barry Roads, South Wales, in ballast, was proceeding at 6 knots, in a strong southwesterly gale when an explosion took place in the after part of the ship. She had struck a mine laid by *U-80*, under Kapitänleutnant Alfred von Glasenapp, commander, some distance south of the Isle of Man, officially reported to be 30 miles north of the Skerries, Anglesey. The ship sank in about 3 minutes, but fortunately the crew of 46 men managed to launch the boats successfully and so abandon ship.

As the master's boat was trying to get clear of the sinking steamship, the master inexplicably seized a rope, which was hanging from the ship, and was dragged overboard and drowned. After searching the vicinity, the boats made for the Isle of Man. On arriving it was found that one of the crew, the quartermaster Chung Hong, was missing. He and Captain Bryden were the only two casualties from the loss of the *Skerries*.

Various positions of loss have been given for the *Skerries*, such as 30 miles north of the Skerries, Anglesey. The official war loss records give the position as 15 miles north-northwest of the Skerries. However, a note was made on the official loss ledger in 1919 stating that if this latter position were correct then the *Skerries* must have hit a floating mine as the minefield itself had been laid 20 miles northeast of the position. A group of naval drifters reported wreckage being picked up 10 miles south of the Chicken Rock, Isle of Man on Sunday 5th November 1916. In reality, it has been proved that the wreck lies in the position where the minefield actually was laid, some 18 miles south of Douglas Head or 26 miles northeast of the Skerries.

## Wreck Site
Latitude 53 51.185 N, Longitude 04 21.730 W

The confirmed wreck of the *Skerries* lies in 53 metres of water. The length of wreck is 120 metres, width 15 metres and height 10 metres. It is orientated 022/202 degrees. The wreck lies on its keel with a 45 degrees list to starboard and the starboard gunnel is the highest point of the wreck. The hull is very broken with the keel facing to the east-southeast. There is a large spare propeller on the deck.

## Paper Sources
British Merchant Ships Sunk by U-Boats in the 1914-1918 War, Tennent
British Vessels Lost at Sea 1914-1918 and 1939-1945, HMSO
Clyde Shipping Company, Harvey and Telford
Lloyd's Register 1916
Lloyd's Wars Losses, the First World War, Casualties to Shipping through Enemy Causes 1914-1918
The National Archives of the UK (TNA): Public Record Office (PRO) ADM 137/2960 and ADM137/599

## Internet Sources
Commonwealth War Graves Commission - www.cwgc.org

**Location**
53 47.383 N
04 25.858 W

Southeast of the Isle of Man

**Vessel**
Steel steamship
Glasgow
ON 102,659
599 tons gross, 237 tons net
1894 by Scott and Sons, Bowling
Triple-expansion engine, 99 rhp,
Muir and Houston, Glasgow
W Robertson, Glasgow
180.0 ft x 29.1 ft x 10.6 ft
54.9 m x 8.9 m x 3.2 m

00.00 hours
18th December 1916

# Disappearance of the steamship *Opal*

The *Opal,* under Captain Donald Martin, master, was bound from Llandulas, North Wales to Belfast with a cargo of limestone on Monday 18th December 1916. She was lost off the southeast coast of the Isle of Man with her twelve crew, including the master, after hitting a mine laid by the German submarine *U-80,* under Kapitänleutnant Alfred von Glasenapp, commander.

The crew of the *Opal* was:

CAMPBELL, Abraham Stewart, second mate
CAMPBELL, Roderick, able seaman
DARRAGH, Thomas, able seaman
GALBRAITH, David, fireman
HANNAH, Hugh, engineer
McDONNELL, Archibald, cook
McKAY, Charles, fireman
McPHERSON, John Shaw, mate
MAGUIRE, Frank, second engineer
MARTIN, Donald, master
MURRAY, John James, ordinary seaman
ROSSBOROUGH, John, fireman

## Wreck Site

Latitude 53 47.383 N, Longitude 04 25.858 W

The probable wreck of the *Opal* lies in 52 metres of water. The length of wreck is 50 metres, width 10 metres and height 6 metres. It is orientated 135/315 degrees. The bow and mid-ships sections are intact, but the stern area has broken off and lies a short distance away from the main wreck.

## Paper Sources

British Merchant Ships Sunk By U-Boats in the 1914-1918 War, Tennent
British Vessels Lost at Sea 1914-1918 and 1939-1945, HMSO
Dictionary of Disasters at Sea during the Age of Steam, Hocking
Lloyd's Register 1916
Lloyd's Wars Losses, the First World War, Casualties to Shipping through Enemy Causes 1914-1918
Steam Coasters, Waine
The National Archives of the UK (TNA): Public Record Office (PRO) ADM137/2960 and ADM137/1250
William Robertson and the Gem Line, Roy Fenton and Philip Robertson
World Ship Society

## Internet Sources

Commonwealth War Graves Commission - www.cwgc.org

**Location**
54 00.362 N
04 33.403 W

2 ½ miles southeast by south
from Langness

**Vessel**
Steel steamship
Sligo
ON 72,499
686 tons gross, 332 tons net
1892 by Messrs John Jones and
Sons, Liverpool
Triple-expansion engine, 187
nhp, Messrs John Jones and
Sons, Liverpool
Sligo Steam Navigation Company
202.6 ft x 29.1 ft x 14.4 ft
61.8 m x 8.9 m x 4.4 m

23.30 hours
19th December 1916

# Sinking of the steamship *Liverpool*

The *Liverpool*, under Captain John Francis Devaney, master, left Liverpool on Tuesday 19th December 1916 at 5.10 pm, bound for Sligo with a large general cargo of merchandise weighing 500 tons. The weather was a bit hazy at the time, but when she reached the Liverpool Bar Lightship it had cleared. The sea was quite smooth. Everything went well until 11.30 pm when a shock was felt and immediately it was ascertained that the vessel had struck a mine.

The position of the vessel at this point was 11 miles southeast by south of the Chicken Rock Lighthouse and the mine had been laid by *U-80*, under Kapitänleutnant Alfred von Glasenapp, commander. Captain Devaney ordered the engines to be stopped and the boats to be launched. He then went forward to inspect the damage, which he concluded was not enough for the vessel to be in immediate danger of sinking. After a head count of the men on board it was quickly surmised that three men were missing. Captain Devaney then made a second journey forward in one of the boats in order to search for the three men, but received no reply. The remainder of the crew then stood off the *Liverpool* in the boats, ready to return if she did not sink.

Captain Devaney went back to the bridge to sound the steam whistle in order to attract the attentions of a steamer coming up behind. With help from the chief mate, he also went forward to get the signal lamps and these were lit and hoisted aloft.

**Above:** The *SS Liverpool* probably in Sligo harbour, Ireland before the war.

**Above:** Captain John Frank Devaney, master of the *SS Liverpool* who is pictured here after being honoured for his bravery on the night that his ship was lost. (Courtesy of his granddaughter Deirdre Murray)

Soon the vessel approached the stricken *Liverpool* and identified herself as the steamship *Ruby*, of Glasgow, under Captain McCawley, bound from Wales to Glasgow with a cargo of stone. The *Ruby* offered to tow the *Liverpool* to Douglas and a hawser was passed to the *Liverpool*. The *Ruby* then commenced towing the *Liverpool* stern first as the head was too deep in the water. After towing for some time Captain McCawley decided to change his plan and tow the *Liverpool* to Belfast instead as the weather had quickly deteriorated, making progress to Douglas impossible. A second hawser was added and towing commenced for a second period. About 5.30 am on Wednesday 20th December, the *Liverpool* was noticed to be taking a bigger list to starboard and Captain McCawley immediately ordered the hawsers to be cut with axes. 10 minutes later, the *Liverpool* disappeared beneath the waves in a position given at the time as 2 ½ miles southeast by south from Langness.

The survivors of the *Liverpool* were:

BANNON, W, fireman, Omeath
BOYD, T, chief engineer, Manchester
BURNS, J, fireman, Liverpool
DEVANEY, John Francis, master, Sligo
KILGALLEN, J, sailor, Rosses Point
McGOWAN, J, steward, Rosses Point
McGOWAN, James, sailor, Rosses Point
McLOUGLIN, Michael, first mate, Raughley
MOFFATT, J, sailor, Sligo
MOFFATT, John, second mate, Sligo
PETRIE, A, sailor, Sligo
SMITH, J, fireman, Omeath
SMITH, J, donkeyman, Armagh
THOMAS, Ivor, second engineer, Rosses Point

The three men who died were:

COSTELLO, J, Sligo
GARVEY, Daniel, winch man, Sligo
GILLEN, J P, the sole passenger on board, Rosses Point

It was the opinion of Captain Devaney that Costello was killed by the force of the explosion, while Garvey and Gillen were drowned, being unable to get through the wreckage. The survivors were landed by the *Ruby* at Clydebank.

A lifebuoy marked with the name of the *"SS Liverpool, of Sligo"*, and a quantity of general wreckage, was washed up near Port St Mary later the same day.

## Wreck Site
Latitude 54 00.362 N, Longitude 04 33.403 W

The confirmed wreck of the *Liverpool* lies in 38 metres of water (the main bell was recovered in 1997). The length of the wreck is 56 metres, width 12 metres and height 5 metres. It is orientated 045/225 degrees. The bow has been completely destroyed by a combination of the initial mine explosion and the impact of the vessel with the seabed. Aft of the bow is the section where the cattle stalls were located and the cargo hold, still full of the merchandise that she was carrying: building materials, crockery, bottled beer and shoes, amongst other items. Most cargo remains in the hold, but is buried deep in the wreckage. The bridge area lies immediately in front of the massive boiler, which forms the highest part of the wreck along with the engine. The engine is an impressive sight rising 5 metres from the seabed. From the engine to the stern is where the passenger accommodation was situated. Finally, the stern section is almost intact down from the original deck level to the keel. It is in this area that pieces of the ship's crockery have been found. The graceful shape of the classic counter stern can be seen, complete with the intact single propeller standing clear of the seabed

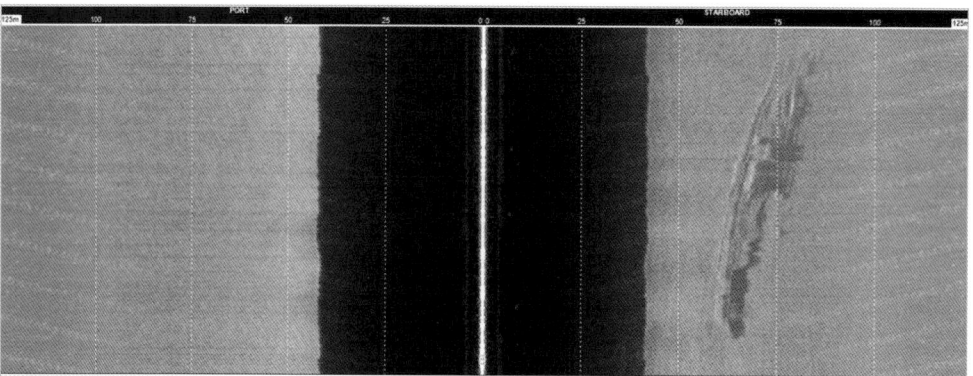

**Above:** Sidescan image of the wreck of the *SS Liverpool.* Her stern is at the bottom of the image with the boiler and engine in the middle of the wreck. Each of these features casts a long "shadow" showing that they rise several metres off the seabed. The bow is at the top of the image and is clearly broken up.

**Above:** One of the two ship's bells recovered by local diver Dave Copley from the wreck of the *SS Liverpool.*

## Paper Sources

British Vessels Lost at Sea 1914-1918 and 1939-1945, HMSO

History of Steam Navigation, Kennedy (1903)

Isle of Man Times 23.12.1916. Manx National Heritage

Lloyd's Register 1916

Lloyd's Wars Losses, the First World War, Casualties to Shipping through Enemy
Causes 1914-1918

Sligo Independent Saturday 30.12.1916.

Sligo Champion Saturday 10.08.1918.

The National Archives of the UK (TNA): Public Record Office (PRO) ADM 137/2960
and ADM137/1250

World Ship Society

# Minefield off the Calf of Man

On Thursday 21st December 1916 information was received of the position of a suspected minefield to the southeast of the Calf of Man. Preparations were immediately made for sweeping which commenced at daybreak on Friday 22nd December when a portion of the area was swept, but no mines were located. The whole of the area was finished by 29th December. The wreck of the *Liverpool* was located and special care taken of the surrounding area, though no mines were found.

**Paper Sources**
The National Archives of the UK (TNA): Public Record Office (PRO) ADM 137/599

**Location**
53 57.000 N
04 40.000 W

6 miles south of Castletown

**Vessel**
Steel steamship
Liverpool
ON 113,476
20,904 tons gross, 13,449 tons net
1901 by Harland and Wolff, Belfast
Quadruple-expansion engine, 1,524 nhp, Harland and Wolff, Belfast
Ocean Steam Navigation Company Limited, James Street, Liverpool (the White Star Line)
680.9 ft x 75.3 ft x 44.1 ft
207.6 m x 23.0 m x 13.4 m

08.58 hours
15th February 1917

# Mining of the steamship *Celtic*

The *Celtic* proceeded from Liverpool at 4.00 am on Thursday 15th February 1917 bound for New York. She was carrying about 1,000 tons of general cargo and had a crew of 160 men. At 5.20 am the Liverpool Bar Lightship was abeam and Captain Bertram Fox Hayes gave orders for a general course of N62W (true) and at 7.00 am gave the order to zigzag.

At 8.58 am, in a fresh easterly wind and hazy conditions, the *Celtic* was in position 53 57 N, 04 40 W, about 6 miles south of Castletown, Isle of Man, when suddenly an explosion occurred under the port bow. Captain Hayes immediately stopped the engines and ordered soundings. The carpenter reported 28 feet 9 inches of water in the forepeak and 30 feet in number one hold. Captain Hayes ordered the bulkhead between numbers one and two holds to be shored and after this work was completed he turned his ship for Liverpool and steamed slowly back arriving there at 8.20 pm the same day.

After hitting the mine the *Celtic* had broadcast a distress message which was intercepted at Holyhead and two trawlers, three armed drifters and two motor launches were dispatched to render assistance but this was not needed by the *Celtic.*

**Above:** *SS Celtic.*

It was thought that the mine was from the group laid in November or December 1916 by *U-80*, under Kapitänleutnant Alfred von Glasenapp, commander, which claimed several other ships in the area including the steamships *Skerries*, *Opal* and *Liverpool*.

## Paper Sources

Lloyd's Register 1916

The National Archives of the UK (TNA): Public Record Office (PRO) ADM137/136

**Location**
54 30.731 N
04 14.815 W

Irish Sea

**Vessel**
Steel steamship
Liverpool
ON 111,362
357 tons gross, 141 tons net
1900 by Ailsa Shipbuilding
Company, Troon
Compound engine, 71 rhp, Ross
and Duncan, Govan
Zillah Shipping and Carrying
Company Limited, Liverpool
(William Savage, manager)
143.3 ft x 24.1 ft x 11.1 ft
43.7 m x 7.3 m x 3.4 m

00.00 hours
10th March 1917

# Disappearance of the steamship
# *G A Savage*

O n the Saturday 10th March 1917, the *G A Savage,* under Captain George H Hardley, master, departed Workington bound for Swansea, laden with a cargo of pitch. She disappeared and it is assumed that she was sunk by a German submarine in the Irish Sea with the loss of her nine crewmen:

CLEARY, Philip, second engineer
HARDLEY, George H, master
HODGSON, Alexander, chief engineer
KRAMMER, Carl Martin, mate
ROBERTSON, A, fireman
THOMAS, Tom, fireman
WALMSLEY, Silas, ordinary seaman
WATTERSON, William Henry, able seaman
WILLIAMS, David, able seaman

William Henry Watterson was from Cregneash, a village in the southwest of the Isle of Man and was only 17 years of age when he died. His father, Henry Watterson, was the master of another of Messrs Savage and Company's fleet of Liverpool coastal cargo steamers.

A wreck to the northeast of the Point of Ayre may possibly be this vessel as the wreck shows evidence of possible torpedo damage. The only vessel lost in the Irish Sea in the war that hasn't been located and matches the details of this wreck is the *G A Savage.* Other sources quote the *G A Savage* being lost off Pendeen Point, South Wales, but her wreck has never been located in that area.

**Above:** *SS G A Savage.*

## Wreck Site

Latitude 54 30.731 N, Longitude 04 14.815 W

The possible wreck of the *G A Savage* lies in 42 metres of water. The length of wreck is 40 metres, width 8 metres and height 7 metres. It is orientated 165/345 degrees with the bow facing south. Sections forward of the boiler are fairly complete with the many hull plates having fallen off the framework. The bow is largely intact and has a large water tank. The hold is empty, without any sign of her cargo. The rear third of the ship has gone through severe trauma. It has an even heavier list to port and at the very stern, the hull, rudder and propeller are lying in a heap. It seems possible that a torpedo may have hit her on the port side abaft the funnel.

Portholes recovered from the wreck were manufactured by Roby's of Rainhill near Liverpool. The maker's stamp is identical to that used on the steamship *Liverpool's* portholes, manufactured in 1892. A ceramic barometer dial recovered by a diver was manufactured by *"Whyte and Thomson, of Glasgow"*. This company traded from 1889 until 1953 but officially became Whyte, Thomson and Company in 1934 although instruments were thus marked from about 1920. Ceramic dials were used in marine barometers from about 1860 to 1910. Thus the date of manufacture would seem to be 1890 to 1910. The *G A Savage* was built in 1900.

## Paper Sources
Isle of Man Examiner Saturday 24.03.1917. Manx National Heritage
Lloyd's Register 1916
Lloyd's Wars Losses, the First World War, Casualties to Shipping through Enemy Causes 1914-1918
Mersey Rovers, R S Fenton
Ramsey Courier Friday 30.03.1917. Manx National Heritage

## Internet Sources
Commonwealth War Graves Commission - www.cwgc.org

**Location**
53 51.494 N
05 01.050 W

9 miles south of the Calf of Man

**Vessel**
Steel steam paddle tug
103 tons gross
1917 by George Brown,
Greenock
Compound diagonal engines,
240 ihp, McKie and Baxter,
Paisley
Inland Transport of the Royal
Engineers
110.0 ft x 20.0 ft x 8.0 ft
33.5 m x 6.1 m x 2.4 m

00.00 hours
10th May 1917

# Foundering of the steam tug *PT1*

The *PT1*, under Captain Donald McLeod, master, left Greenock at 10.00 am on Wednesday 9th May 1917 bound ultimately for the war in Mesopotamia (corresponding to modern day Iraq) and carried a crew of nineteen men. When 9 miles south of the Calf of Man on Thursday 10th May 1917, she commenced to take water in rapidly, presumably as the result of a mechanical failure and the crew were ordered to take to the lifeboats.

The starboard boat got clear with eight of the crew, but the port boat became jammed under the port paddle box and capsized, the occupants being thrown into the water. Five were picked up, but six men were drowned.

The survivors were in the open lifeboat for about 1 ½ hours before they were picked up by a trawler and taken into Peel. Later, Sapper Chateris died from exposure as a result of having been immersed in the sea.

The men who died were:

ATKIN, Edward, corporal, 233149
CHATERIS, sapper
GREEN, John Henry, sapper, 272050
MacLEOD, Donald, lieutenant
STEEL, John Edmund, sergeant, 202339
SWANGER, T S, lance corporal, 157563
YOUNG, Charles, sapper, 265251

The men who survived were:

BROWN, J, second lieutenant
CASPER, C, second lieutenant
EVANS, E, second lieutenant
FIFE, corporal
HOCKRIDGE, sapper
KERR, M D, lieutenant
LUCAS, J, sapper
McDONALD, J, sapper
O'DONNELL, sapper
SEDDON, A H, second lieutenant
TEASDALE, J, sapper
WOODS, G, sapper

The *PT1* was originally ordered by Royal Indian Marine with the name *T44* along with a series of tunnel screw tugs, but during construction it was decided to give the paddle tugs their own serial numbers, commencing *"PT"*. When completed the *PT1* was under the jurisdiction of the Inland Transport of the Royal Engineers.

**Wreck Site**
Latitude 53 51.494 N, Longitude 05 01.050 W

The possible wreck of the *PT1* lies in 82 metres of water. The length of wreck is 25 metres, width 5 metres and height 4 metres. It is orientated 000/180 degrees. The wreck may be partially buried and probably lies on a muddy seabed.

**Paper Sources**
Isle of Man Governor's Papers 9485, Manx National Heritage
The Isle of Man and the Great War, Sargeaunt
World Ship Society

**Internet Sources**
Commonwealth War Graves Commission - www.cwgc.org

# The Unrestricted Submarine Campaign Begins

Vice-Admiral Sir John Jellicoe was appointed First Sea Lord on 3rd December 1916 with specific instructions to defeat the U-Boat menace. Four days later, David Lloyd George replaced Herbert Asquith as Prime Minister. One of his first actions was to dismiss Arthur Balfour as First Lord and replace him with Sir Edward Carson. The new team of Jellicoe and Carson set up an anti-submarine division under Rear Admiral Alexander Duff. The Royal Navy's best people were to concentrate on the fight against Germany's U-Boats.

By late 1916 Germany was being reduced to near starvation due to the Allied blockade and it was commonly believed that the United States of America would soon enter the war against Germany. Therefore, pressure for a second unrestricted U-Boat campaign increased and Admiral Henning Holtzendorff was again one of its main proponents. He estimated that 600,000 tons of Allied shipping could be sunk each month and if this was maintained for just 5 months Britain would be forced to sue for peace.

A conference was called at Pless on 8th January 1917 and Chancellor Theobald von Bethmann-Hollweg finally bowed to the inevitable. Later in January 1917, the Kaiser issued the fateful edict: *"I order the unrestricted submarine campaign to begin on 1st February with the utmost energy."*

The campaign developed hesitantly at first as if the submarine commanders were unwilling to fully unleash the potential of their U-Boats. However, any doubts over the U-Boats effectiveness were soon banished as April 1917 was the peak of the *"killing time"* with 354 ships sent to the bottom of the sea in just that 1 month. The Allies had so far failed to find an answer to the U-Boat threat, and even though the United States of America had finally entered the war on 6th April 1917, the outlook was bleak. Vice-Admiral W S Sims of the US Navy advised his government that German submarines were winning the war, an opinion shared by Ambassador Walter Page who wrote, *"What we are witnessing is the defeat of Britain."* Food reserves were reduced to a dangerously low level and rationing was introduced.

With ships being sunk quicker than they could be built the Admiralty made the warning that Britain was to lose the war in November 1917 unless a means of defeating the U-Boat menace was found. Jellicoe, in a memorandum to the War Cabinet on 23rd April 1917, warned that, *"the situation calls for immediate action."*

One such action taken was the introduction of the convoy system in which a large number of ships would sail together to a destination and could be effectively defended by a comparatively small number of escorting warships. Convoys had been used quite early on in the war, in the coal trade to northern France, for instance, but the lack of suitable warships for escort duty had delayed the introduction of a more widely adopted convoy system.

The decision to finally adopt the convoy system was approved by Jellicoe, based on the proposals by Admiral Duff, on 27th April 1917. During May, the first escorted ocean convoy left Gibraltar for England and arrived safely. Shipping losses began to decline but the loss rate was still unsustainable and morale of the Mercantile Marine was seriously weakened. Fortunately the Allies played their cards close to their chests and Germany was not aware of the real effectiveness of its U-Boat campaign and just how close Britain was to surrendering.

The U-Boat campaign had little impact in the waters around the Isle of Man until the latter part of 1917 when paradoxically losses of Allied shipping had halved since its peak in April 1917. The reasons for this are not totally clear. The risks to U-Boats operating in the confines of the Irish Sea were comparatively greater than in more open areas of sea such as the Western Approaches. Perhaps U-Boat commanders felt that they needed to accept the increased risk in order to hunt for targets outside of the main convoy systems. In the Irish Sea they found ships sailing independently of convoys and ships which were sailing from ports to their convoy mustering stations or vice versa. Ships falling into these categories made comparatively easier targets than ships sailing in a heavily defended convoy.

During this period of the war, there were two significant losses of ships from the Royal Navy: *HMS Champagne* in October 1917 and *HMS Stephen Furness* in December 1917. Both ships were torpedoed off the west coast of the Isle of Man with heavy loss of life.

**Location**
54 19.500 N
05 05.500 W

12 miles northwest of Peel

**Vessel**
Steel steamship
Argostoli
2,430 tons gross
1885 by E Withy and Company,
Hartlepool
Triple-expansion engine, 225
nhp, T Richardson and Sons,
Hartlepool
E M Michalitsianos, Bordeaux
302.1 ft x 38.1 ft x 20.2 ft
92.1 m x 11.6 m x 6.2 m
Ex Stella
Ex Lakythra

18.30 hours
24th July 1917

# Sinking of the steamship *Mikelis*

On Tuesday 24th July 1917, the Greek steamship *Mikelis,* under Captain Gerasimis Frengopoulos, master, on charter to the French Government, was bound from Bilbao for Glasgow, laden with 3,500 tons of iron ore. The conditions were calm and foggy, and at 6.30 pm in position 54 19.5 N, 05 05.5 W, approximately 12 miles northwest of Peel, she was apparently torpedoed by a German submarine, later attributed to *U-69,* under Kapitänleutnant Ernst Wilhelms. However, neither the submarine nor torpedo was observed by the captain or crew of the *Mikelis.* At the time the torpedo supposedly hit, the *Mikelis* was steaming on a north-northeast course at 8 knots, but was not zigzagging. The explosion was in her number four hold on the port side.

By 6.40 pm as the ship was sinking fast, Captain Frengopoulos gave the order to abandon ship and the crew of 22 men boarded the boats. The patrol boat *HMS P18* was about 5 miles distant off the *Mikelis'* port quarter and very soon arrived in the vicinity of where the *Mikelis* finally foundered at 7.00 pm. The crew of the *Mikelis* were transferred from the small boats to *HMS PC61* and were landed at Milford Haven the following day.

The following accounts are taken from a confidential report by the Deputy Chief Constable, J Quilliam on the Isle of Man:

*"Mr Cowell, skipper of a Peel fishing boat, reported that yesterday when 12 miles northwest of Peel, he sighted a large quantity of wreckage including a raft which he caused to be*

*examined, and on which were found only two cats which he took to Peel. There was no sign of any living persons. He is satisfied that a large vessel had been sunk and her name was the Teuabbhwiae of Mike v H Z. He also stated that one of HM Patrol boats came there and made an examination."*

*"I have seen the skipper of a fishing boat. He said the wreckage was very thick and extended for 3 miles. There must have been a terrific explosion. The vessel was Greek and the cats appear to be the sole survivors."*

The crew of the *Mikelis* was:

| | |
|---|---|
| CHRISTIDIS, L, chief engineer | LOULYOS, A, fireman |
| FRENGOPOULOS, Gerasimis, master | MAVROGIANIS, D, able seaman |
| FRENGOPOULOS, Gerasimos, second officer | NERATYIS, E, fireman |
| FRENGOPOULOS, Spiros, chief officer | OLIVIERO, M, mess room boy |
| GOULANDRIS, A, fireman | PETRATOS, S, able seaman |
| GREGOS, P, able seaman | PETROPOULOS, E, donkeyman |
| ISOURIS, M, fireman | PRODOMAS, E, fireman |
| KATHARIS, L, boatswain | SCOLIDIS, D, steward |
| KOUTOS, T, second engineer | SIRIGOS, M, able seaman |
| KRISTIS, M, fireman | SMARAGILIS, G, cook |
| LEISKARIS, N, able seaman | ZAFIRAKY, D, third engineer |

There remains some doubt over whether the *Mikelis* was actually torpedoed and she may have sunk after an internal explosion. The last contact with *U-69* was on 11th July 1917 and she was lost with all 40 hands some time after this date. Some records suggest *U-69* did not go missing in the Irish Sea until *after* 24th July 1917. If a torpedo did sink the *Mikelis* then it could well have been fired from *U-69*.

**Wreck Site**
Latitude 54 19.500 N, Longitude 05 05.500 W

The wreck of the *Mikelis* has not been located. She may be the unknown wreck located at 54 23.083 N, 05 06.955 W which lies at a depth of 112 metres.

**Paper Sources**
Isle of Man Government Office Papers 9485, Manx National Heritage
Lloyd's Register 1917
Lloyd's Wars Losses, the First World War, Casualties to Shipping through Enemy Causes 1914-1918
Shipbuilders of the Hartlepools, Spaldin
The National Archives of the UK (TNA): Public Record Office (PRO) ADM137/1362

**Location**
54 06.000 N
05 04.000 W

9 miles west-northwest of the
Calf of Man

**Vessel**
Monmouth class armoured
cruiser
9,800 tons displacement
1902 by William Beadmore and
Company, Govan
Triple-expansion engines,
22,000 ihp
British Admiralty
463.5 ft x 66.0 ft x 25.0 ft
141.3 m x 20.1 m x 7.6 m

01.00 hours
25th July 1917

# Attack on

# *HMS Berwick*

Between midnight on 24th July 1917 and 0.40 am on 25th July *HMS Berwick* had been steaming in very thick fog on a southerly course to clear the dangerous area to the west of the Calf of Man. Speed had been reduced on the order of Captain W F Blunk from 20 knots to 10 knots and navigation lights with a reduced visibility of 1 mile had been switched on. The ship cleared the fog bank and two vessels were sighted to starboard at an approximate range of half a mile. Both had their navigation lights on and were showing steaming and port bow lights to *HMS Berwick*. At this moment *HMS Berwick* increased her speed to 12 knots being the first intended increase towards resuming the original speed of 20 knots. In view of the crossing position of the other vessels Captain Blunk decided to keep the navigation lights on until *HMS Berwick* was clear of the other steamers.

A few minutes later the nearest steamer commenced flashing signals, using an extremely bright electric flashing light, but the letters were not intelligible so *HMS Berwick* did not answer the message. The steamers made Captain Blunk suspicious. At 0.48 am the leading vessel of the two steamers had closed on *HMS Berwick* and was approximately off her beam, with the second steamer stationed behind her. *HMS Berwick* increased her speed to 15 knots intending to draw ahead. At the same moment a white light, judged to be the stern light of a steamer, was sighted directly ahead, and in view of the positions of all three ships, Captain Blunk decided to port across the bows of the first two steamers, and under the stern of the vessel ahead. At 0.54 am *HMS Berwick* had swung off half a point when Captain Blunk gave the order to steady south by west (true), to observe how the white light drew. From the way it rapidly approached it seemed evident to Captain

Blunk that the white light belonged not to an overtaken steamer but to a small fishing vessel. *HMS Berwick* therefore steadied to pass it close to her port bow.

By 1.00 am *HMS Berwick* was in position 54 06 N, 05 04 W, approximately 9 miles west-northwest of the Calf of Man, and the white light was directly abreast of her forebridge at a distance of 70 yards. Captain Blunk had just given the order to resume her original course of south (true) when a pair of torpedoes was observed. The officers on the bridge then made out the white light to be that on a submarine and they saw the torpedoes leaving the tubes. Captain Blunk immediately ordered full speed ahead both engines and hard a port with the helm in order to bring the white light astern. The torpedoes passed close to *HMS Berwick's* stem. The submarine had fired a second pair of torpedoes and the action by *HMS Berwick* to turn hard a port meant that these torpedoes passed very close to her starboard side, the nearest of the pair being only 20 feet from *HMS Berwick*. Fine handling of the helm by the navigation officer, Lieutenant H T Bennett, under the instructions of Captain Blunk undoubtedly saved *HMS Berwick* from disaster.

*HMS Berwick* did not have her stern guns on standby when the incident occurred so she was unable to open fire on the submarine during the short interval when there was a clear target. Due to the high speed of his vessel, Captain Blunk had thought it unnecessary to have gun cover aft.

**Above:** *HMS Berwick.* (Courtesy of the Imperial War Museum)

It was the opinion of Captain Blunk that the decoy ships intended to crowd his vessel so that she would pass the submarine on her port side on a more or less known course. The hurried change in the deposition of their attack necessitated him to port *HMS Berwick* at 0.52 am, and by passing the starboard side of the enemy submarine, his ship escaped being torpedoed.

The only U-Boat potentially operating in the Irish Sea at this time was *U-69*, under Kapitänleutnant Ernst Wilhelms. *U-69* may have torpedoed and sunk the steamship *Mikelis* off Peel the previous day. The last contact with *U-69* was on 11th July 1917 and she was lost with all 40 hands some time after this date. Some records suggest *U-69* did not go missing in the Irish Sea until after 24th July 1917.

## Paper Sources

The National Archives of the UK (TNA): Public Record Office (PRO) Office ADM137/1362

**Location**
54 10.656 N
05 03.703 W

Between the Isle of Man and
Northern Ireland

**Vessel**
Steel steamship
5,360 tons gross
1895 by Harland and Wolff,
Belfast
Triple-expansion engines, 568
nhp, Harland and Wolff, Belfast
British Admiralty
421.0 ft x 48.8 ft x 33.0 ft
128.4 m x 14.9 m x 10.1 m
Ex Oropesa

# Sinking of
## *HMS Champagne*

The steamship *Oropesa* was built for the Pacific Steam Navigation Company but was taken over by the Admiralty in November 1914, for service in the World War One as an auxiliary cruiser. She was armed with six 6-inch guns and two 6-pounders. The ship was a unit of the 10th Cruiser Squadron under Rear Admiral Sir Dudley de Chair, and while patrolling between Scotland and Norway sank a German submarine off Skerryvore Lighthouse south of Tiree in March 1915. In 1917 she was lent to the French navy and her name changed to *Champagne*, but she retained her British crew.

During the war, the approaches to the major port of Liverpool were patrolled by a number of ships of the Royal Navy. Amongst these was *HMS Champagne*. On Monday 8th October 1917 the German submarine *U-96*, under Kapitänleutnant Heinrich Jeß, was reported in the Irish Sea, about 30 miles off the mouth of the Mersey, moving northwest towards the Isle of Man.

Captain Percy G Brown of *HMS Champagne* decided to avoid *U-96* when she left Liverpool early on Tuesday 9th October 1917, by sailing west along the coast of North Wales and then across the Irish Sea well towards Ireland, before turning northeast, putting the Isle of Man to starboard. Meanwhile, *U-96* found shelter from the north-northwest gale in the lee of Spanish Head in the south of the Isle of Man, eventually leaving this haven, heading towards the Irish coast.

At 6.10 am in position 54 17 N, 05 10 W (other positions researched include 6 miles off St John's Point, County Down and 8 miles southwest of the Calf of Man) whilst she was

**Above:** *HMS Champagne* when called the *Oropesa*.

zigzagging and on a course of N 21 E (magnetic), speed 13 knots, she was struck in the engine room on the starboard side by a torpedo fired from *U-96*. The lookout on the starboard after gun saw a periscope and gave the order *"Close–up"*. HMS *Champagne* was struck almost immediately by the torpedo and the periscope disappeared.

The engineer officer of the watch was blown to pieces and there were several casualties in the engine room. The ship's company automatically went to action stations; the leading torpedo man put the depth charges to safe and reported to the captain. Some of the confidential papers were locked up in steel safes by the decoding officers and the remainder were destroyed. All steam was cut off by the explosion. The senior Warrant Telegraphist reported to Captain Brown that the wireless gear, both main and auxiliary, was out of action and two Warrant Telegraphists assisted by the electrician then endeavoured to repair the auxiliary set, but both later lost their lives in their devotion to duty.

The main engines were stopped by the explosion and the ship could not go astern and lost her way almost at once in the force 5 to 7 west-northwest wind. The First Lieutenant asked Captain Brown to give the order to abandon ship, but Captain Brown said, *"No, not yet, as the ship may float for a considerable time and we may bag the submarine if he comes up."* Almost immediately there was a second explosion on the port side in the fore part of the after well deck after a second torpedo struck her. Captain Brown at once gave the order to abandon ship. *HMS Champagne* had remained on an even keel up to this point but then began to settle rapidly.

The boats, with the exception of the collapsibles, were got away smartly, although difficulties were encountered in the rough seas. The First Lieutenant left in the last of the boats, the upper deck at that point being awash, and he only left upon Captain Brown's order.

**Above:** The final moments of *HMS Champagne* as she breaks in two shortly before sinking.

Four men, able seaman Oliver Ward RNVR, able seaman Ryan RNVR, leading seaman Watkins RNR and leading seaman W J Cox RNR, volunteered to stay behind to man the foremost pair of guns just after the second explosion. Ward saw a submarine, the *U-96*, come to the surface about 300 to 400 yards away from the port beam. The port foremost 6-inch gun was fired at once, the shell going just over the submarine. The submarine dived at once and the gun was reloaded and a tube inserted. The men stayed by their gun as the ship settled and only Cox survived.

The collapsibles were stored abreast of the other boats which had to be lowered first and were generally hard to manhandle without the aid of a steam winch. This resulted in only two of them being launched. Sub-Lieutenants Nalder and Hyslop RNR, the officers of the boats, endeavoured to get further collapsibles launched and Captain Brown ordered Petty Officer W J Ware RFR to get spars to lever them over the side. At about 6.30 am the port boat was half over when *HMS Champagne* was struck again by a third and final torpedo on the port side of the funnel, the explosion being what can only be described as tremendous. *HMS Champagne* broke completely in two and sank within 30 seconds, the port collapsible fell over the side and some men managed to scramble into it. The starboard collapsible floated bottom up and a few men clung on to it, while others got on board rafts and wreckage which had floated to the surface.

Owing to the heavy weather and masses of floating wreckage, the boats experienced great difficulty in picking up the survivors. Captain Brown and leading seaman Con (one of the gun crew) were left in the water and managed to stay afloat by grabbing hold of a large empty biscuit tank before they were picked out of the sea by the boat commanded by Lieutenant Bingham RNR at some time between 7.30 am and 8.00 am. The boat then hoisted her sail and ran before the northwesterly wind followed by a second boat.

The seas were rough but the two boats made Port Erin at about 11.30 am where they landed and Captain Brown telephoned the coastguard in order that they could wireless for help. The remaining boats were too overloaded to sail into port but were eventually towed into Port St Mary by two steam trawlers at 1.30 pm. Peel's lifeboat, *Mayhew Medwin,* was launched at 12.25 pm to search for life rafts and 2 hours later, one was spotted with 21 men on board. Because of the heavy sea, it was a very difficult task to transfer the exhausted men onto the lifeboat. Only after a valiant effort was the lifeboat able to return home. Once the survivors were ashore, the *Mayhew Medwin* resumed her search, this time without success. In the meantime, two rafts, Sub-Lieutenant Nalder being on board one, were picked up by merchant vessels and the survivors landed at Liverpool and Manchester. The casualties amongst the saved men were slight with only two men injured. Four Manxmen were on board *HMS Champagne.* They were James Keenan, ship's carpenter, Albany Street, Douglas; James Kinley, Hatfield Grove, Douglas; William Christian, of Port Erin; and Frank Moore, Bradda, Port Erin.

Out of a total compliment of 34 officers and 271 men, five officers and 53 men were found to be missing. Considering the weather, distance from land, the shortness of time between first attack and *HMS Champagne* sinking, Captain Brown thought it was extremely fortunate that so many of her crew were saved. At the Court Martial proceedings of 12th November 1917, Captain Brown praised the excellent behaviour of his officers and crew during the sinking and the hospitality of the people of the Isle of Man for caring for the survivors. Captain Brown commented, *"The ship went down with a portion of her guns manned, and ready to fire, and the traditions of the service were upheld."*

Of the 58 officers and crew who were stated to be missing in 1917, only 47 are listed on the Commonwealth War Graves Commission's database and they are:

ALCOCK, William, trimmer, MMR 903292
BAILEY, Frederick Maurice, warrant telegraphist, RNR

BIRD, George, fireman, MMR 900906

BOYER, George, stoker first class, (RFR/B/4817) SS/117671 (Dev)

BRADSHAW, Edward, assistant baker, MMR 898669

BRADY, Joseph, trimmer, MMR 900536

BROWN, James, trimmer, MMR 896891

CLAYTON, Joseph, trimmer, MMR 898589

COHEN, Bernard, fireman, MMR 889327

COMPTON, Thomas, trimmer, MMR 877686

COOPER, Joseph, trimmer, MMR 883628

DEAKIN, Albert, trimmer, MMR 926588

DENT, George, able seaman, RNVR Bristol Z/4641

EDWARDS, Charles William, fireman, MMR 864951

HARDEN, Walter Marshall, steward, MMR 44403

HEMINGWAY, Wilfred O, telegraphist, RNVR Mersey Z/1263

HENRY, Reginald, able seaman, RNVR Tyneside Z/8974

HYSLOP, John William, sub-lieutenant, RNR

JOHNSON, Alfred, trimmer, MMR 891758

JOURNEAUX, Wilfred Redfers, boy first class, J/48373

KING, Stanhope, petty officer first class, (RFR/A/2518) 128561 (Dev)

LAYDEN, William, able seaman, RNVR Clyde Z/7108

LEONARD, Frank, able seaman, RNVR London Z/4241

McGLASSON, William Smith, seaman, RNR 6483A

McLEOD, Arthur, engineer sub-lieutenant, RNR

MANGAN, John, trimmer, MMR 926592

MARSHALL, William A, ordinary seaman, RNVR Mersey Z/3326

MAWHINNEY, James, trimmer, MMR 933111

NAJAF, Muhammad, assistant cook, MMR 898678

PECKHAM, William, greaser, MMR 585516

RYAN, John, able seaman, RNVR London Z/4133

SHAW, John, seaman, RNR 7469A

SIMS, Horace W, chief writer, MMR 877537

STANNARD, Charles Edward, warrant telegraphist, RNR

STOCK, Albert, fireman, MMR 905943

STOTT, James, stoker first class, (RFR B/4709) SS/106061 (Dev)

SUCCAMORE, William J, trimmer, MMR 931462

SWEETMAN, Peter, fireman, MMR 909968

THOMAS, William E, leading seaman, RNR D/1948

THOMPSON, Jacob John, trimmer, MMR 914422

WAKEFORD, Charles, assistant paymaster, RNR

WALTER, Eric Douglas, able seaman, RNVR Mersey Z/957

WARD, Oliver, able seaman, RNVR Bristol Z/4587

WATERSON, William Benjamin, chief cook, MMR 847681

WATKINS, Joseph, leading seaman, RNR C/1774

WEST, William E, able seaman, RNVR London Z/3991

WHITWAM, Arthur Edward, armourer's crew, M/16731 (Dev)

## Wreck Site

Latitude 54 10.656 N, Longitude 05 03.703 W

The probable wreck of *HMS Champagne* lies in 99 metres of water. The length of wreck is 83 metres, width 15 metres and height 12 metres. Owing to its location in deep water northwest of the Calf of Man the wreck probably lies on a muddy seabed.

## Paper Sources

Dictionary of Disasters at Sea during the Age of Steam, Hocking
Lloyd's Wars Losses, the First World War, Casualties to Shipping through Enemy Causes 1914-1918
The Isle of Man and the Great War, Sargeaunt
The Lifeboats of Peel, Quilliam
The National Archives of the UK (TNA): Public Record Office (PRO) ADM137/3696, ADM137/344 and ADM137/942

## Internet Sources

Commonwealth War Graves Commission - www.cwgc.org
Great War Forum - 1914-1918.invisionzone.com

**Location**
53 56.877 N
04 44.652 W

South of the Isle of Man

**Vessel**
Steel steam trawler
ON 108,463
161 tons gross, 63 tons net
1897 by Mackie and Thomson,
Glasgow
Triple-expansion engine,
307 nhp, Muir and Houston,
Glasgow
British Admiralty
104.2 ft x 20.5 ft x 10.7 ft
31.8 m x 6.3 m x 3.3 m

00.00 hours
10th October 1917

# Disappearance of
# *HMT Waltham*

Before the war, the *Waltham* was owned by the Consolidated Steam Fishing and Ice Company Limited, of Grimsby. The *Waltham* was requisitioned by the Admiralty in December 1914 and armed with a single 6-pound gun.

Whilst on Admiralty Service, *HMT Waltham*, under James Mair, master, disappeared off the Isle of Man on Wednesday 10th October 1917 and was presumed at the time by the Admiralty to have been torpedoed by a German submarine with the loss of her thirteen crewmen.

The following letter reported on her loss:

*"HM Naval Base, Larne Harbour*
*25 October 1917*
*No 2039/24*

*Sir,*
*I regret to have to report that I fear that HM Trawler Waltham No. 689 attached to this base, has been lost with all hands. This vessel was specially disguised and was manned by volunteers from men in vessels attached to this Base.*

*On Wednesday 10th of October, information was received that an enemy submarine was working outside our area to the south in the vicinity between St John's Point and the Isle of Man. HM Trawler proceeded on the same day to the vicinity where the submarine was reported, and has not been heard of since. In the ordinary course she should have returned to this base, after at most 10 days, but no news has been received of her up to the present.*

*Several vessels were reported sunk by enemy submarines in the vicinity where she may have been working, and I regret to state that in all probability she was attacked and sunk by an enemy submarine. Search has been made of this vessel, and information requested from all Coast Guard stations and Bases within the area she was working, and no information is reported as to her having been seen, or trawler wreckage."*

The following is a list of officers and crew, all of whom were volunteers:

CAMPBELL, Duncan, able seaman, RNR 689DA
FEWSTER, Charles Frederick, trimmer, RNR 4246TS
HOLLAND, Michael Daniel, deckhand, RNR 2788DA
MAIR, James, skipper, RNR 1570WSA
MARSH, Robert Wright, trimmer, RNR 5300TS
RICHARDSON, Edmund, deckhand, RNR 8304DA
SMITH, John, trimmer, RNR 1923TS
STEPHEN, Peter Strachan, deckhand, RNR 4860DA
STEWART, James White, deckhand, RNR 4009DA
STRACHAN, Robert, engineer, RNR 1829ES
TOLAN, William, trimmer, RNR 2639TS
WEBSTER, William John, second mate, RNR 4812DA
WILSON, David, deckhand, RNR 3276DA

**Above:** Platter recovered from the wreck of the *HMT Waltham* by local diver Ed Bimson. (Courtesy of Ed Bimson)

German records made public since the end of World War One include the log book of the German mine laying submarine *UC-75*. The records show that the *UC-75* was the submarine referred to in the letter above. Oberleutnant zur See Johannes Lohs drew charts of his mission route through the Irish Sea on the 4th and 5th October 1917 and the positions of where he laid his mines, including three mines to the south of the Calf of Man about 6 to 8 miles off the coast. U-Boats did not intentionally torpedo trawlers; they weren't considered worth a torpedo. Nor is the sinking of *HMT Waltham* attributed to any U-Boat in the German official history of U-Boat operations. Therefore, *HMT Waltham* undoubtedly hit one of the mines laid by *UC-75* and sank south of the Calf of Man some 6 to 8 miles off the coast with the loss of all hands.

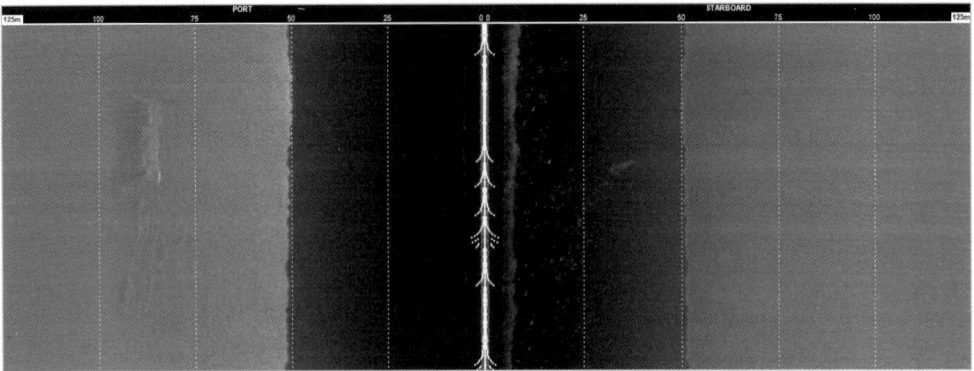

**Above:** Sidescan image of the wreck of *HMT Waltham*. A large shadow can be seen coming from the largely intact stern section. The two thirds of the ship ahead of the boiler can be seen to be largely flat on the seabed.

**Wreck Site**
Latitude 53 56.877 N, Longitude 04 44.652 W

The wreck of *HMT Waltham* lies in 51 metres of water. The length of wreck is 45 metres, width 7 metres and height 7 metres. It is orientated 045/225 degrees. The wreck was first dived in April 1997 and thought to be that of a steam trawler of about 100 to 120 feet in length. A large winch was observed in front of the open bridge. A triple-expansion engine and boiler were found to be at the stern of the vessel. The stern section lies on its port side and is largely intact but the wreck was completely broken ahead of the boiler and the hold and bow sections were largely flat to the seabed. The wreck was assumed to be the *Waltham* in 1997 following this dive.

However, further dives cast doubt on this identification and the wreck was misidentified as the steam tug *Vivid* also lost in this vicinity. It was not until more dives after 2004 that it was confirmed that the wreck was a screw steamer. Dives in 2010 confirmed the 1997 details. In addition, evidence of the supports for the gun platform can be seen at the stern of the wreck. To date no bell or other object to make an absolutely 100 per cent identification has been recovered but the author is certain that the wreck is that of *HMT Waltham*.

**Above:** Diver Ed Bimson next to the rudder on the wreck of *HMT Waltham*.

## Paper Sources

British Vessels Lost at Sea 1914-1918 and 1939-1945, HMSO
Lloyd's Wars Losses, the First World War, Casualties to Shipping through Enemy Causes 1914-1918
The National Archives of the UK (TNA): Public Record Office (PRO) ADM 137/1362
World Ship Society

## Internet Sources

Commonwealth War Graves Commission - www.cwgc.org
Great War Forum - 1914-1918.invisionzone.com
uboat.net - www.uboat.net

**Location**
53 43.000 N
05 04.000 W

21 miles southwest of the Calf
of Man

**Vessel**
Steel steamship
Liverpool
ON 110,611
9,399 tons gross, 6,176 tons net
1899 by Armstrong, Whitworth
and Company Limited,
Newcastle
Triple-expansion engine, 701
nhp, Wallsend Slipway Company
Limited, Newcastle
F Leyland and Company
Limited, Liverpool
482.0 ft x 57.1 ft x 32.8 ft
147.0 m x 17.4 m x 10.0 m

06.25 hours
3rd November 1917

# Attack on the steamship *Atlantian*

The *Atlantian*, under Captain Thomas Chadwick, master, with a crew of 63 men, left Norfolk, Virginia on Tuesday 16th October 1917 bound for Liverpool with 10,000 tons of general cargo, including cotton, copper, steel billets and oil. She crossed the Atlantic as part of a convoy of 24 ships.

The convoy passed Rathlin Island on the evening of Friday 2nd November. The Liverpool section of the convoy then broke off and proceeded down the Irish coast as far as the South Rock Light Vessel, when the weather came on thick and the *Atlantian* lost sight of the Irish lights and the other ships in her section. The wind was blowing hard from the southeast, a considerable sea was running and her speed was limited to 9 knots on a course of south-southwest (magnetic).

At 6.25 am on Saturday 3rd November, the *Atlantian* was in position 53 43 N, 05 04 W still steering south-southwest, but not zigzagging due to the poor visibility. The chief and third officers were on the bridge with lookouts in the crow's nest, on the forecastle head, one on each side on the saloon deck and a further lookout on the after bridge with the gunner. Suddenly, there was a huge explosion near the stern caused by a torpedo which had approached the ship on the port beam. It had been seen too late to take any evasive action.

The explosion blew the rudder away, but did not damage the propellers. The stern section of the hull was badly damaged and the gun was thrown from its mounting. The gunner and lookout were thrown from the gun platform and the lookout sustained head and internal injuries. The engines were at once stopped to ascertain the damage. They were found to be in proper working order and the ship was not making any water. The *Atlantian* then commenced steering south at 6 knots using her propellers to steer. A distress call was sent out, *"Ship torpedoed"* and an answer was received from Seaforth. For whatever reason, *UC-75*, under Oberleutnant zur See Johannes Lohs, did not press home her attack and no second torpedo was fired.

The *Atlantian* passed Point Lynas at about noon and when eastward of Great Orme's Head was met by the tug *Cartmel* at 4.50 pm. The tug took the *Atlantian* in tow and proceeded towards Liverpool Bar, where the two ships arrived at 10.00 pm and anchored to await further assistance. The tender *Magnetic* arrived at 11.30 pm and remained alongside the injured steamer until 5.00 am on Sunday 4th November when the *Cartmel* once again commenced the tow and proceeded up the Mersey with the assistance of several other tugs. The *Atlantian* was docked at 2.00 pm.

## Paper Sources

British Vessels Lost at Sea 1914-1918 and 1939-1945, HMSO
Lloyd's Register 1916
Lloyd's Wars Losses, the First World War, Casualties to Shipping through Enemy Causes 1914-1918
The National Archives of the UK (TNA): Public Record Office (PRO) ADM137/1362

**Location**
53 54.000 N
04 56.000 W

10 miles south-southwest of the Calf of Man

**Vessel**
Steel steamship
Dundalk
ON 107,003
794 tons gross, 327 tons net
1899 by A and J Inglis, Glasgow
Triple-expansion engine, 283
nhp, A and J Inglis, Glasgow
Dundalk and Newry Steam
Packet Company, Dundalk (S J
Cocks, manager)
236.0 ft x 32.1 ft x 15.2 ft
72.0 m x 9.8 m x 4.6 m

10.00 hours
6th December 1917

# Attack on the steamship *Dundalk*

The *Dundalk*, under Captain Hugh O'Neill, master, left Liverpool at 3.00 am on Thursday 6th December 1917 bound for Dundalk, having received route instructions from the Shipping Intelligence Officer at Liverpool. At 10.00 am the vessel was about 10 miles south-southwest of the Calf of Man, steering northwest (magnetic) at 11½ knots but not zigzagging when a craft was observed by the mate (who was in charge of the bridge) just before the port beam and fully 5 miles distant. Not being sure of the identity of the craft, the *Dundalk* carried on her course, but when the craft was off the *Dundalk's* port quarter the mate could make out that it was in fact a submarine. The helm was at once ported to bring the submarine astern and simultaneously the submarine opened fire, but the shot fell a long way short.

The *Dundalk* made all speed with her engines and speed increased to 14 knots. She made short zigzags and headed northeast towards the Isle of Man. The submarine continued to chase, firing her deck gun sometimes fairly quickly and then in intervals of 5 or 6 minutes. After the first shot by the submarine the *Dundalk* opened fire with her 90 mm gun at maximum range, but the shot fell short of the enemy. Two more shots were fired but both fell well short so firing was ceased. The crew of the *Dundalk* then threw three smoke boxes overboard which caused enough smoke to interfere with the aim of the German gunners. Twenty minutes later, three more boxes were deployed. Later, when more smoke boxes were tried they would not light so smoke was made from the *Dundalk's* port cowl, which created a volume of smoke and enveloped the *Dundalk*.

The chase continued until about 11.30 am, when the submarine appeared to be dropping astern and apparently gave up the chase. The submarine fired 52 shot and shell altogether, but none of them struck the *Dundalk,* though one shell exploded on the starboard side, damaging the lifeboat there.

After the submarine disappeared the *Dundalk* carried on her way to Peel, where she arrived at 2.00 pm, having signalled to the lookout station at Spanish Head as she passed.

## Paper Sources

British Vessels Lost at Sea 1914-1918 and 1939-1945, HMSO
Lloyd's Register 1917
The National Archives of the UK (TNA): Public Record Office (PRO) ADM137/1362

**Location**
54 13.309 N
05 02.367 W

15 miles west by north of
Contrary Head

**Vessel**
Steel steamship
Newcastle
ON 129,753
1,712 tons gross, 745 tons net
1910 by Irvine's Steamboat
and Dry Dock Company, West
Hartlepool
Triple-expansion engine, 359
nhp, Richardsons, Westgarth
and Company Limited,
Hartlepool
British Admiralty
290.0 ft x 37.0 ft x 16.0 ft
88.4 m x 11.3 m x 4.9 m

16.15 hours
13th December 1917

# Sinking of
# *HMS Stephen*
# *Furness*

On the 1st December 1914, the *Stephen Furness* was hired as a depot ship by the Admiralty for war purposes. Later in May 1915, her role changed to that of a store carrier before in March 1916 she was converted to an Armed Boarding Steamer.

*HMS Stephen Furness* left Lerwick at 2.00 pm on Tuesday 11th December 1917 under the command of Lieutenant Commander T M Winslow, RNR. She was proceeding to Liverpool, under orders issued by the Rear Admiral at Lerwick, where she would undergo repairs.

At 4.15 pm on Thursday 13th December 1917, whilst zigzagging at a speed of 13 knots and 15 miles west by north of Contrary Head, Isle of Man, she was struck by a torpedo on her starboard side, between the bridge and the funnel, smashing numbers one and three boats. The torpedo had been fired from the German submarine *UB-64*, under Kapitänleutnant Walter Gude.

Lieutenant P S Simmonds was in command on the bridge when the explosion occurred. He gave the order through the voice pipe to ring the alarm bell and gave a rough training to the fore gun. He then tried to get into communication with the after gun but could get no reply due to the voice pipe to the gun being destroyed. Lieutenant Commander Winslow appeared on the bridge and asked Lieutenant Simmonds if the explosion had been caused by a mine or torpedo. Lieutenant Simmonds replied that it had been a torpedo and pointed to the track which led away from the ship abaft the beam. Captain

Winslow ordered the forward gun to be trained in the direction of where the submarine had launched her attack. The gun layer of the foremost gun replied that the gun had jammed and could not be trained. Captain Winslow ordered Lieutenant Simmonds down to the wireless room to see if a distress message could be broadcast. However, the wireless cabin had also been destroyed in the explosion of the torpedo.

The torpedo had breached the hull of the ship at about the position of the athwart ship bulkhead, under the forebridge, between number two hold and the boiler room. As a result of the damage and there being no watertight bulkhead between the collision bulkhead forward and the after end of the engine room, she filled rapidly, dipping by the bow. The order was given by Lieutenant Commander Winslow to abandon ship. The chief boatswain's mate came on the bridge and asked if there were any orders. Lieutenant Simmonds told him to pipe *"Abandon ship"*, which he did as he went around the boat deck several times. The officers and crew attended their muster stations in an orderly fashion. Captain Winslow told Lieutenant Simmonds to go to his boat which was number five on the starboard side. It was impossible for him to get along the starboard side of the deck owing to the wreckage of numbers one and three boats. He went around the port side and saw that all the port boats were manned and were in the act of being lowered. He stepped into number five boat but before it could be lowered, *HMS Stephen Furness* suddenly sank by the head taking all the boats with her. As she sank she rose almost perpendicularly in the air. Less than 3 minutes had elapsed since the torpedo had first struck.

Number five boat capsized immediately on striking the water and was dragged down with the ship, the men being underneath. Several men managed to scramble from under the lifeboat, including Lieutenant Simmonds, as they were not wearing lifebelts. By this time they were some considerable depth under water but Lieutenant Simmonds rose to the surface and managed to swim to a raft. He was unable to climb onto the raft for some time due to an injury to his leg, but finally succeeded with assistance from a fireman named Charles Saddington. The majority of the crew did not escape and were taken down with the steamer.

At 6.30 pm the navigation lights of a trawler were observed and the survivors managed to attract her attention. The trawler was the *Elite*, returning from escort duty from Belfast and steaming to Holyhead. She picked up the twelve men, searched about for more survivors for 2 hours then proceeded to her destination of Holyhead. The *Elite* picked up the survivors in position 54 15 N 05 07 W. *HMS Stephen Furness* sank with the loss of six officers and 92 ratings.

At the Court Martial proceedings held on the 1st February 1918 at HM Navigational School, Dockyard, Portsmouth, no blame was attributed to Lieutenant Simmonds or any of the survivors. It was recorded that the conduct of the officers and crew of *HMS Stephen Furness* was in accordance with the best traditions of His Majesty's Service.

**Above:** *HMS Stephen Furness* before the war.

The six officers and 92 ratings who died were:

ATKINSON, John Ernest, boy first class, RN J/50189(PO)
BACH, Thomas, trimmer, MMR 517845
BARKER, Arthur, engineer's storekeeper, MMR
BARLOW, Thomas Walter, signalman, RNVR Bristol Z/3863(D)
BELL, Andrew, greaser, MMR 827797
BLORE, George William, ship's steward, RN 344752
BOBBINS, William, petty officer, RN 118764
BOND, Charles, fireman, MMR 851255
BROWN, John, engineer, Lieutenant RNR
BROWN, John David, greaser, MMR 580219
BUCKETT, Richard Henry, (DSM) assistant steward, MMR 919848
BUCKROYD, John Edwin, able seaman, RN J/28417(PO)
BUNTING, John, greaser, MMR
BURKE, Joseph, greaser, MMR 895673
BURNS, Thomas, chief cook, MMR 661506
CAMP, George Robert, ship's cook, MMR 790965
CATTERMOLE, Christopher Stanley, boy first class, RN J/56621 (PO)
CHURCHHOUSE, Arthur F, telegraphist, RNVR Tyneside Z/5506
CLAYTON, Fred, able seaman, RNVR Tyneside Z/10204
COX, Valentine, boy first class, RN J/43284
CRANG, Walter, able seaman, RNVR Bristol Z/1486 (D);
DALEY, James, able seaman, RNVR KX/344
DAVIES, Sidney Lewis, trimmer, MMR 908669
DEELEY, Walter, able seaman, RNVR Bristol Z/3950 (D)
DUPREY, Alfred Frank, signalman, RNVR London 3/1923
DYOTT, Kenelm Mitchill, Temp/Surgeon, RN

ETCHELLS, William, able seaman, RNVR Mersey Z/940 (D)

EVANS, Vernon Arthur Martin, trimmer, MMR 606961;

EVANS, William, able seaman, RN 161370

FOXON, Harold Lewis, able seaman, RNVR Wales Z/2506 (D)

FRISWELL, John Roderick Thomas, sick berth attendant, RN M/4681

GAHAN, Thomas, trimmer, MMR 882873

GALVIN, Joseph, trimmer, MMR 919543

GEORGE, Alastair Farquhar, able seaman, RNVR Clyde Z/7118

GOULD, William Henry Felix, Temp/Sub-Lieutenant, RNR

GROVES, Walter William, fireman, MMR 803936

HALL, Joseph William, able seaman, RNVR Bristol Z/9158

HAMMOND, Harry George, distilling greaser, MMR 882495

HAWORTH, William, wireman second class, RN M/19828 (PO)

HESELTINE, Willie, armourer's crew, RN M/7833 (PO)

HODGKINSON, Francis George, petty officer first class, RN 154453 (10)

HOPKINS, James, assistant steward, MMR 919843

HOWSE, Thomas John Albert, fireman, MMR 814969

HUNTER, William Thomas, sailors' mess man, MMR

KELLY, William Joseph, cook, MMR 766986

LAWES, H B, able seaman, RNCVR VR/2614

LOVEDAY, Henry, chief petty officer, RN 144288

McCALLUM, David Crawford, ordinary seaman, RNVR Clyde Z/8220

McDONALD, James, fireman, MMR

McDONALD, Lawrence, fireman, MMR 683636

McGREGOR, Alexander Thomson, Temp/Engineer Lieutenant, RNR

McINTOSH, Karl, able seaman, RNVR Clyde Z/7550

McKENZIE, John, fireman, MMR 866084

McKENZIE, John McDonald, greaser, MMR 912798

MacRAE, Alexander, able seaman, RNVR Clyde Z/7516

MANSELL, Herbert, distilling greaser, MMR 140295

MEEHAN, Henry Leo, able seaman, RNCVR VR/2598

MEREDITH, Arthur Reginald, boy first class, RN J/44147

MORRISON, John, seaman, RNR 3486/A

MUDIE, John Fitzgerald, leading signalman, RNR 3591A

MULLANEY, John, able seaman, RNVR Clyde Z/4224

OAKES, Albert, private, RMLI PO/18286

PALMER, George Walter, private, RMLI PO/15895

PATIENCE, John William, petty officer, RNR 2923/C

RAINFORD, Thomas Henry, fireman, MMR 687088

RATCLIFFE, Robert Francis, able seaman, RNVR Wales Z/2756 (D)

REDFORD, Ralph, trimmer, MMR 895534

REED, Cuthbert Reveley, private, RMLI, PO/17455

RHODES, Arthur Leslie, ship's steward assistant, RN M/14236

RITCHIE, Henry, seaman, RNR 4678A (PO)

ROBINSON, John, fireman, MMR 708613

ROBINSON, John, able seaman, RNVR Bristol Z/4937 (D)

ROGERS, Henry Richard, fireman, MMR 606957;

ROMANS, William Franklyn, able seaman, RNCVR VR/2653

SHIRLEY, William, fireman, MMR 903163

SKINNER, John, seaman, RNR 5282A (PO)

SMITH, Alfred Albert, private, RMLI PO/18226

SMITH, Francis, trimmer, MMR

SOREL-CAMERON, Herbert Augustus, Acting Temp/Lieutenant, RNR

SOUTHALL, Sidney, assistant cook, MMR 871756

SOUTHWELL, Alfred, steward, MMR 897024

STEVENS, George Philip Lancelot, donkeyman, MMR 102563

STEVENS, Sidney James, private, RMLI PO/9089

STONE, Ernest William, ordinary seaman, RNVR Bristol Z/5347

TALMEY, W F, able seaman, RN 170445

TAYLOR, Francis Thomas, trimmer, MMR 884286

TAYLOR, James Henry, private, RMLI PO/11170

THORPE, James, trimmer, MMR

TUCKER, Leonard Francis, able seaman, RN 227581(PO)

WALLIS, John Edwin, assistant steward, MMR 919845

WATT, R D, able seaman, RNCVR VR, 2532

WENBORNE, William, fireman, MMR 679029

WHITE, William John, able seaman, RN SS, 16(D)

WIGMORE, A E, able seaman, RNCVR VR/2524

WILLIAMS, Frank David, able seaman, RNVR Clyde Z/5982(PO)

WILLIAMSON, Edward Thomas, sergeant, RMLI, PO/13798

WINGATE, John William, ordinary seaman, RN J/42198

WINSLOW, Thomas Maitland (RD), Lieutenant Commander, RNR

WOODHOUSE, James, leading seaman, RNR 3300B

WYBROW, Thomas James, private, RMLI PO/9917

Some historical sources give the casualties as six officers and 95 ratings. However, there is evidence that three men left the ship at Lerwick so weren't on *HMS Stephen Furness* at the time of her loss which explains the discrepancy with the records held by the Commonwealth War Graves Commission from which the list above was derived.

The 12 survivors were:

CHALK, Frederick, able seaman, RNCVR VR/2652

CLARK, R S, Temp/Engineer Sub-Lieutenant, RNR

GREER, William, telegraphist, RNVR Clyde Z/2759

HARRIS, George, assistant steward, MMR 789783

LYNGNANE, James Arthur, petty officer, RN 194711

McAVOY, Lawrence, carpenter, MMR 919846

OLSSON, John, greaser, MMR 702838

PRAGNELL, Herbert Clifton, boy first class, RN J/44676

SADDINGTON, Charles, fireman, MMR 817735

SHERINGHAM, H W, Temp/Acting Paymaster, RNR

SIMMONDS, P S, Temp/Lieutenant, RNR

WINFIELD, J C, Temp/ Engineer Sub-Lieutenant, RNR

**Above:** Graves of sailors from *HMS Stephen Furness* in Douglas Borough Cemetery.

## Wreck Site

Latitude 54 13.309 N, Longitude 05 02.367 W

The probable wreck of the *HMS Stephen Furness* lies in 116 metres of water. The height of the wreck is 6 metres. It most likely lies on a muddy seabed.

## Paper Sources

British Merchant Ships Sunk by U-Boats in the 1914-1918 War, Tennent
British Vessels Lost at Sea 1914-1918 and 1939-1945, HMSO
Dictionary of Disasters at Sea during the Age of Steam, Hocking
Lloyd's Register 1917
Lloyd's Wars Losses, the First World War, Casualties to Shipping through Enemy Causes 1914-1918
The National Archives of the UK (TNA): Public Record Office (PRO) ADM137/136, ADM 137/344, ADM 137/942 and ADM1/8514/46
World Ship Society

## Internet Sources

Commonwealth War Graves Commission - www.cwgc.org

**Location**
53 44.345 N
05 08.099 W

25 miles southwest of the
Calf of Man

**Vessel**
Steel steamship
Mauriupol
3,849 tons gross, 2,348 tons net
1896 by Tyne Iron Steam Boat
Company, Newcastle
Triple-expansion engine, 357
nhp, North Eastern Marine
Engineering Company Limited,
Newcastle
F C Svorono and E Di Pollone
350.0 ft x 47.0 ft x 17.2 ft
106.7 m x 14.3 m x 5.2 m
Ex Tropic

04.10 hours
2nd January 1918

# Sinking of the steamship *Nadejda*

The Russian steamship *Nadejda*, under Captain John Kraukle, master, left Keret in the White Sea on Wednesday 21st November 1917 on charter to the Russian Government, laden with 249 standards of timber, bound for Barry Roads at which point she would await further orders. She called at Lerwick, Kirkwall, Loch Ewe and Loch Foyle and, on passing Red Bay, County Antrim, received the latest instructions from a patrol yacht as to the course to be steered across the Irish Sea on the final leg of her voyage to Barry Roads off the coast of South Wales.

By 4.10 am on Wednesday 2nd January 1918, the *Nadejda* passed the Chicken Rock and at 6.10 am she was in approximate position 53 40 N, 05 15 W proceeding at a speed of 10 knots on a steady and not zigzagging, south-southwest ¼ west (magnetic) course. The weather was fine but cloudy with a light northeasterly wind. All her navigation lights were off and all other lights on the ship screened. Suddenly, a torpedo slammed into the port side of her number four hold and exploded breaking the propeller shaft, blowing the number four hatch cover clean off and destroying some of her derricks.

The *Nadejda* at once began to settle by the stern and her crew went to their boat stations and lowered the two lifeboats. 33 men climbed into the boats, but Captain Kraukle and two of the officers remained on board for a further 10 to 15 minutes before they too abandoned ship by using the jolly boat to go out to the starboard lifeboat.

The two lifeboats remained in the vicinity of the sinking *Nadejda* until daybreak. Suddenly, a periscope from the *U-19,* under Kapitänleutnant Johannes Spieß, appeared standing about 7 feet clear of the surface of the sea. It sped along, passing so close to the one of the lifeboats that the crew could have hit it with an oar. The submarine then sped away to the northeast and disappeared from sight. At this point the steamer's stern was awash and the *U-19* must have assumed that she would soon sink. However, her cargo of buoyant wood was delaying the process.

The steamship *Portwood*, under Captain Lawson, master, left Milford Haven at 1.00 pm on Tuesday 1st January 1918 bound for Liverpool and at 8.45 am the next day when in position 53 35 N, 05 11 W observed two lifeboats in the water about 8 or 9 miles on the *Portwood's* port bow making sail in a strong northerly wind in the direction of the South Stack. Captain Lawson then steered towards the lifeboats and picked up the occupants of the *Nadejda's* port lifeboat which was in charge of the chief officer, Ernst Janson, and contained 18 other men. The occupants of the starboard boat, which was in charge of Captain Kraukle, were rescued by the Spanish steamer *Udala Mendi* which landed them at Penzance on Friday 4th January.

The steamship *Enda*, Captain John Robert Godfrey, master, proceeded from Dublin at 9.25 am on Wednesday 2nd January 1918 bound for Garston in water ballast of 240 tons and manned by a crew of 13 with two gunners. At 1.30 pm the same day she was approximately 24 miles east of the Baily Lighthouse at Howth, Ireland when she spotted a large steamer with her stern almost submerged and apparently abandoned. Captain Godfrey assembled a small volunteer crew who got on board one of the *Enda's* lifeboats and rowed over to the abandoned steamer. On reaching the casualty they decided not to attempt to board her owing to the heavy seas. The abandoned steamer was assumed to have been the Russian steamer *Nadejda*.

## Wreck Site
Latitude 53 44.345 N, Longitude 05 08.099 W

The possible wreck of the *Nadejda* lies in 72 metres of water. The length of wreck is 90 metres, width 25 metres and height 8 metres. It is orientated 120/300 degrees. The wreck is upright and intact with bows northwest.

## Paper Sources
Dictionary of Disasters at Sea during the Age of Steam, Hocking
Lloyd's Register 1917
Lloyd's Wars Losses, the First World War, Casualties to Shipping through Enemy Causes 1914-1918
The National Archives of the UK (TNA): Public Record Office (PRO) ADM137/1514
World Ship Society

# The Main Offensive

The main offensive of the unrestricted U-Boat campaign in the waters around the Isle of Man occurred from February through March and into the first few days of April 1918 with nearly half of all the incidents of the war (28 out of 61) occurring in just the span of 2 months. This was part of a renewed offensive by the U-Boat fleet to make a decisive impact against Allied shipping and to swing the war in Germany's favour. February 1918 saw a world tonnage of 318,900 tons sunk by U-Boats and/or mines. The total for March was 342,500 tons, April 278,700 tons and May 295,500 tons.

However, by the spring of 1918 the losses of U-Boats by mines, net defences, surface patrols, and sea planes had almost reached breaking point and the effectiveness of the U-Boat campaign could not be maintained during the summer of 1918. It is very noticeable that U-Boat activity tailed off significantly in the waters around the Isle of Man during this period. By January 1918 the quality of U-Boat crews was also beginning to suffer a decrease in quality as the old volunteer system had broken down and both inexperienced officers and men were drafted into the submarine service as new U-Boats were commissioned.

Two new factors were beginning to contribute significantly to the increased effectiveness of the Allies to combat the U-Boats. Firstly, April 1918 saw the introduction of the first electronic devices for anti-submarine warfare being deployed in the waters around the Isle of Man. *HM Yacht Helga* used a hydrophone in an attempt to destroy a U-Boat a few miles off the Calf of Man on 4th April although it was unsuccessful. Secondly, the impact of patrol ships from the United States Navy was beginning to make an impact. The destroyer *USS Downes* was in action against a U-Boat south of the Isle of Man on 20th February.

**Location**
54 01.875 N
03 56.790 W

20 miles southeast of
Maughold Head

**Vessel**
Steel steamship
Liverpool
ON 137,527
427 tons gross
1916 by Lytham Steam Boat and
Engineering Company Limited,
Lytham
Triple-expansion engine, 88
rhp, Lytham Steam Boat and
Engineering Company Limited,
Lytham
Zillah Shipping and Carrying
Company Limited (G A Savage
Limited, managers)
142.2 ft x 26.0 ft x 11.5 ft
43.4 m x 7.9 m x 3.5 m

11.45 hours
7th February 1918

# Sinking of the steamship *Limesfield*

On Thursday 7th February at 11.45 am, the tide being 4 hours on the ebb, the weather hazy, the wind from the west-southwest blowing fresh and a rough sea from the west, the *Limesfield* was proceeding on her voyage from Belfast to Preston, laden with cotton waste. In a position about 20 miles southeast of Maughold Head, a shell suddenly burst above the bridge. The master and mate were on the bridge at the time and fortunately escaped injury. On looking out on the starboard side of the *Limesfield* the master, Captain William Galbraith, observed the German submarine *UB-57*, under Oberleutnant zur See Johannes Lohs, about 1 mile distant, which continued to fire more shells at the *Limesfield*.

The master ordered the small boat to be lowered and after destroying confidential papers by fire, he left the steamer along with the rest of the crew. After they had rowed a short distance Oberleutnant Lohs of the *UB-57* signalled them to stop and coming alongside the small boat questioned Captain Galbraith as to the name of his vessel and the nature of the cargo that she was carrying. The last he saw of his vessel was that she had taken fire and it was assumed that the submarine continued shelling her until she foundered.

After rowing for about 6 hours the crew were picked up by the Fleetwood fishing trawler *Reliance* and landed at Fleetwood at 4.00 am on Friday 8th February 1918.

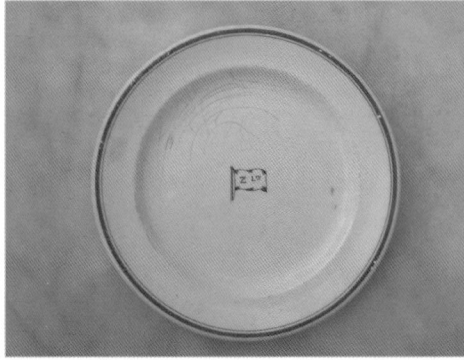

**Above:** Plate recovered from the wreck of the *SS Limesfield*.

## Wreck Site

Latitude 54 01.875 N, Longitude 03 56.790 W

The confirmed wreck of the *Limesfield* lies in 41 metres of water (the bell was recovered in 1996). The length of wreck is 44 metres, width 8 metres and height 5 metres. It is orientated 022/202 degrees. The wreck is intact and upright with the bow facing to the north-northeast.

**Above:** The author diving on the wreck of the *SS Limesfield*.

## Paper Sources

A History of Shipbuilding at Lytham, Dakres

British Vessels Lost at Sea 1914-1918 and 1939-1945, HMSO

Lloyd's Wars Losses, the First World War, Casualties to Shipping through Enemy Causes 1914-1918

Ramsey Courier Tuesday 12.02.1918. Manx National Heritage

The National Archives of the UK (TNA): Public Record Office (PRO) ADM 137/1514

World Ship Society

## Location

54 01.627 N
03 53.853 W

35 miles west-northwest of the
Liverpool Bar Lightship

## Vessel

Steel steamship
Ramsey
ON 121,247
212 tons gross, 79 tons net
1905 by George Brown and
Company, Greenock
Compound engine, 40 nhp,
Colin Houston and Company,
Glasgow
Ramsey Steamship Company
Limited, Ramsey
110.0 ft x 22.1 ft x 8.3 ft
33.5 m x 6.7 m x 2.5 m
Ex Starling

13.50 hours
7<sup>th</sup> February 1918

# Sinking of the steamship *Ben Rein*

On Thursday 7th February 1918, the *Ben Rein*, under Captain John Cowley, master, was on a journey from Liverpool to Belfast with a cargo of 150 tons of soap. At 1.50 pm the crew heard firing in the distance when about 35 miles west-northwest of Liverpool Bar Lightship. As the haze lifted they saw, about a mile distant, the three-masted steamer *Limesfield* being attacked by the German submarine *UB-57*, under Oberleutnant zur See Johannes Lohs. The crew of the *Ben Rein* put on full steam to try to escape but the U-Boat, now finished with the other ship turned its attention to the *Ben Rein*, firing a volley as a signal to stop. The *Ben Rein* duly stopped and the crew got the small boat out, whilst the submarine started firing at the steamer, but clear of the small boat. The first direct hit on the steamer went through the captain's room and the third shot got the boiler.

After this the submarine drew close to the small boat and the commander of the submarine put questions to the crew of the *Ben Rein* as to the nature of the cargo and her destination. The commander then ordered them, politely and in good English, to go back aboard the *Ben Rein* and to take off a portion of the cargo. However, at this point the steamer had caught fire and it was impossible to obey his command. The submarine left and shortly afterwards the steamship rose vertically in the water and sank.

Two of the engine room crew had only dungarees as protection from the cold winter weather and so one of the other men gave his coat to fireman T Corlett. In addition, a tarpaulin was cut up to form a lugsail and a piece of it was used to wrap engineer J Lewin up in.

For the first 4 to 5 hours of their journey to safety there was a heavy sea running, but afterwards the sea was calm. During this time they heard more gunfire and this would seem to have been aimed at the third steamship sunk that day by *UB-57*, the *Ardbeg*. Later, her crew of seven men was rescued by the steamer *Norman* and landed in Whitehaven at 2.00 am on Friday 8th February.

The crew of the *Ben Rein* were:

BRIDSON, J, mate, Peel
CARRAN, H J, seaman, Port Erin
CORLETT, T, fireman, St Jude's
CORTEEN, H, engineer, Douglas
COWLEY, John, master, Port St Mary
COWLEY, J W, seaman, Port St Mary
LEWIN, J, engineer, Peel

**Above:** *SS Ben Rein.* (Courtesy of Manx National Heritage)

**Wreck Site**

Latitude 54 01.627 N, Longitude 03 53.853 W

The confirmed wreck of the *Ben Rein* lies in 39 metres of water (the bell inscribed with her original name of *"Starling"* was recovered in 1997). The length of wreck is 37 metres, width 8 metres and height 4.5 metres. It is orientated 045/225 degrees. The wreck is intact and upright with the bow facing to the southwest. The superstructure, which was originally at the rear of the vessel, has collapsed to deck level. The long single hold still contains the cargo of soap in wooden crates. Even though the soap has gone the crates still contained the wrapping papers when the wreck was dived in the late 1990s. Several large pieces of wreckage lie off the bow.

**Paper Sources**

British Vessels Lost at Sea 1914-1918 and 1939-1945, HMSO
Isle of Man Times Saturdays 09.02.1918. and 16.02.1918. Manx National Heritage
Lloyd's Register 1918
Lloyd's Wars Losses, the First World War, Casualties to Shipping through Enemy Causes 1914-1918
Ninety Years of the Ramsey Steamship Company Limited, Gray and Fenton
Ramsey Steamship Company
War Casualty Book World War 1 Volume 3
World Ship Society

**Vessel**
Steel steamship
Glasgow
ON 111,260
227 tons gross, 85 tons net
1900 by Scott and Sons, Bowling
Compound engine, 35 rhp, Muir
and Houston Limited, Glasgow
Glasgow Steam Coasters
Company Limited (Hendry,
McCallum and Company,
managers)
117.0 ft x 21.5 ft x 9.4 ft
35.7 m x 6.6 m x 2.9 m

14.30 hours
7th February 1918

# Sinking of the steamship *Ardbeg*

The *Ardbeg*, under Captain William Hugh McCoffey, master, left Warrington for Larne with a cargo of 160 tons of soda ash on Thursday 7th February 1918. The cargo was being shipped by agents Brunner Mond and Company, of Winnington, for the Aluminium Company, of Larne.

At 2.30 pm the tide being about half flood, the weather hazy, wind blowing fresh from the west-southwest and with a heavy sea from the west, the *Ardbeg* was about 32 miles north ½ east (magnetic) from the Liverpool Bar Lightship, when the master, who was on the bridge, observed two German submarines about 2 ½ miles ahead and about 1 ½ miles apart. One submarine was then seen to submerge and the other, *UB-57*, under Oberleutnant zur See Johannes Lohs, circled around as if to ascertain whether the *Ardbeg* was armed and then fired a shell, which missed the *Ardbeg*. A second shell was fired which struck the starboard boat and carried away the steering gear. *UB-57* fired three more shots, with one striking the steamer aft and then fired a further six shots as the *Ardbeg's* crew clambered in to the remaining lifeboat. A few more shots were fired before the lifeboat was ordered alongside the submarine. Questions were asked by Oberleutnant zur See Lohs of *UB-57* concerning the name of the ship and nature of her cargo. The *Ardbeg's* crew were then told to leave their ship and the submarine continued to fire at the steamer until she sank at 4.00 pm.

The *Ardbeg's* crew reached the Selker Light Vessel near Millom, Cumbria at 9.15 pm and were taken off by *HMS Touchwood* at 8.15 am the following morning and landed at Fleetwood.

## Wreck Site
Latitude 54 02.217 N, Longitude 03 45.828 W

The confirmed wreck of the *Ardbeg* lies in 36 metres of water. The length of wreck is 37 metres, width 8 metres and height 4 metres. It is orientated 135/315 degrees. The wreck is intact and upright with the bow facing to the southeast.

## Paper Sources
British Vessels Lost at Sea 1914-1918 and 1939-1945, HMSO
Lloyd's Register 1918
Lloyd's Wars Losses, the First World War, Casualties to Shipping through Enemy Causes 1914-1918
The National Archives of the UK (TNA): Public Record Office (PRO) ADM 137/1514
World Ship Society

**Location**
53 50.000 N
05 30.000 W

25 miles southwest of the
Chicken Rock

**Vessel**
Steel steamship
ON 109,420
1,030 tons gross
1913 by Caledonian Steam Boat
and Engineering Company
Limited, Dundee
Triple-expansion engine, 225
nhp, Caledonian Steam Boat and
Engineering Company Limited,
Dundee
British Admiralty
230.2 ft x 35.6 ft x 14.4 ft
70.2 m x 10.9 m x 4.4 m
Ex Jurassic

13.20 hours
11th February 1918

# Sinking of
# *HMS Cullist*

P rior to the war, the *Westphalia* was owned by the Leith, Hull and Hamburg Steam Packet Company (Currie, James and Company, of Leith, managers) before she was hired by the Admiralty as an Royal Fleet Auxiliary store carrier, and she operated in this role between October 1914 and June 1916. The *Westphalia* was converted to a Special Service Ship or "*Q-ship*" in March 1917 and renamed *HMS Cullist*, being armed with one 4-inch gun, two 12-pounder guns and two 14-inch torpedo tubes.

At 1.20 pm on Monday 11th February 1918 the "*Q*" ship *HMS Cullist*, bound from New York for La Pallice, La Rochelle, France, laden with steel ingots, was at the time steaming on a southerly course down the Irish Sea, Drogheda being about 25 miles to the westward (approximately 25 miles southwest of the Chicken Rock). The officer of the watch and the look-out men were at their posts, and Lieutenant Commander S H Simpson RN was walking up and down the deck. Suddenly, from nowhere, the track of a torpedo was seen approaching. The ship was struck between the engine-room and number three hold. Lieutenant Commander Simpson was hurled into the air and came down on to the edge of the deck injuring his arm. Realising the condition of *HMS Cullist*, he ordered his men to abandon ship, but such was the duty of the crew in remaining at action stations until the last moment that many of them were drowned; in less than 2 minutes *HMS Cullist* had gone to the bottom, taking five officers and 38 men with her. The survivors, numbering

27 men, were left swimming about or keeping alive on a small Carley float, a very shallow raft, painted Navy grey, and usually supplied with a paddle such as found in a Canadian canoe.

The German submarine *U-97*, under Kapitänleutnant Hans von Mohl, when half a mile astern of where *HMS Cullist* sank, came to the surface and rapidly approached. She stopped and picked up two men, inquiring after the captain and observing the other survivors through glasses. Having abused the survivors by words and gestures, the *U-97* made off to the southward. After swimming about for some time, Lieutenant Commander Simpson was pulled on to the Carley float. It was a bleak February afternoon, and here were a few men able to keep from death by joining hands on the crowded raft. As the hours went on, the usual trying thirst assailed them and with it the fatal temptation to drink the sea-water, but the captain wisely and sternly prevented this. How long they would be left crowded in the raft, cold and miserable, no one knew; it was obvious that they could not last out indefinitely.

But just as it was getting dusk, about 6.00 pm, a trawler was seen. The Canadian paddle was held high enough to make it easier for the trawler to recognize them. It was a patrol trawler, for the gun was visible. In a few moments they would be rescued. But the sopping-wet survivors were horrified to see the trawler manning her gun and training it on to the raft. Fearing that the trawler would attack, Lieutenant Commander Simpson shouted to the men to *"Sing at the top of your voices."* So they sang *"Tipperary"* with all the strength they had left. A slight pause was followed by the trawler's master dismissing the gun's crew and then heading his trawler towards the survivors as quickly as her engines would go round. They were picked up by the trawler which they now knew as the *James Green* and taken into Kingstown (now Dun Laoghaire), where they landed about 10.00 pm.

But why had the *James Green* prepared to attack the raft? Her crew had sighted something in the half-light which resembled a submarine, and on examining it again it still resembled such a craft. There was the conning tower painted grey, and there was the periscope too. It was only when the unmistakable sound of British voices chanting *"Tipperary"* reached their ears that they looked again and found that the *"periscope"* was the Canadian paddle, and the *"conning-tower"* was the men linked together on the grey Carley float.

The men killed on *HMS Cullist* were:

BARTELL, John, donkeyman, MMR 569832
BATES, Leonard, ordinary seaman, RN J/31917
BROWNE, Ernest, officer's steward second class, RN L/10031
CARR, Horatius Hartley, ordinary seaman, RN J/56109
COCKBURN, John, trimmer, MMR 916106

COOK, Percy, fireman, MMR 867709

CORVAN, Patrick Lawrence, fireman, MMR 914396

DEAN, Stanley Edwin, ordinary telegraphist, RNVR, London Z/5705

DOUBLEDAY, George Hambrook Dean, DSC, lieutenant, RNR

GARWOOD, Sidney George, ordinary seaman, RN J/34085

GAY, Albert Stephen, leading seaman, RN 235675

GILLAN, Michael, fireman, MMR 863035

GULLY, Lewis Vincent, engineer sub-lieutenant, RNR

HALL, Frederick, officer's steward second class, RN 362323

HINDLEY, Robert Muir, paymaster, RNR

HOBAN, Richard Edward, ordinary seaman, RN J/54372

JELFS, Raymond Victor John, able seaman, RN J/14804

JOINSON, Joseph Henry, trimmer, MMR 903388

KERSLEY, Walter, able seaman, RN SS/6249

LAMB, John, shipwright, RN M/26794

LEARY, Jerimiah, able seaman, RN 228557

LEWIS, Joseph, fireman, MMR

LYCETT, William Ernest, ordinary seaman, RN J/43431

McCARTHY, Dennis, ordinary seaman, RN J/39317

McFADDEN, Robert, trimmer, MMR 904076

McIVOR, John, fireman, MMR 911817

McROBBIE, William, corporal, RMLI PO/16334

MacKINNON, Neal Shaw, engineering lieutenant, RNR

MARIS, Christopher Reginald, leading telegraphist, RN J/12544

MARTIN, Alfred, able seaman, RN J/24076

PATTEN, Tom Franklin, cook's mate, RN M/20827

RICH, Herbert Henry, leading cook's mate, RN M/3700

ROBILLIARD, Ernest, leading seaman, RN 234437

SHEATHER, Alfred Reginald, petty officer, RN J/6418

SHOEBOTTOM, Samuel Joseph, armourer's crew, RN M/7163

SMITH, William Edward, able seaman, RN J/7882

STEBBINGS, Henry Edwin, private, RMLI PO/14835

TURNER, Thomas Thompson, officer's steward third class, RN L18905

WALTER, Hubert Norman, leading seaman, RN J/8922

WHITCHURCH, Frederick Thomas, signalman, RN J/7432

WHITE, George Harold Edward, ordinary seaman, RN J/34670

WHITTON, David John, surgeon probationer, RNVR

WOODALL, Ernest, painter, RN M4929

**Wreck Site**

Latitude 53 50.000 N, Longitude 05 30.000 W

The wreck of *HMS Cullist* has not been located.

**Paper Sources**

British Merchant Ships Sunk by U-Boats in the 1914-1918 War, Tennent

British Vessels Lost at Sea 1914-1918 and 1939-1945, HMSO

Der Handelskrieg Mit U-Booten

Lloyd's Register 1918

Lloyd's Wars Losses, the First World War, Casualties to Shipping through Enemy Causes 1914-1918

Q Ships and Their Story, E. Keble Chatterton (1922)

The National Archives of the UK (TNA): Public Record Office (PRO) ADM 137/1514 and ADM137/755


**Internet Sources**

Commonwealth War Graves Commission - www.cwgc.org

**Location**
53 50.000 N
04 45.000 W

South of the Isle of Man

**Vessel**
Steel destroyer
1,072 tons displacement
1913 by New York Shipbuilding,
Camden
Direct drive turbines with triple-
expansion cruising engines,
16,000 shp
US Navy
305.3 ft x 31.2 ft x 10.5 ft
93.1 m x 9.5 m x 3.2 m

21.30 hours
20th February 1918

# USS Downes attacks a German submarine

On Wednesday 20th February 1918, the destroyer *USS Downes* was escorting a mail steamer when at 11.00 am a message was received from *USS Parker* that a submarine had been heard 6 miles north of Bardsey Island, off northwest Wales. Full speed was made to head for the location. At 12.20 pm a further message was received from *USS Parker* stating that the submarine now appeared to be in position 5 miles north-northwest of Bardsey Island. On reaching the position a retiring search was commenced covering the northern section of the search area with *USS Parker* and *USS Burrows* covering the southern and western sectors.

At 4.40 pm *USS Downes* responded to a SOS signal and arrived at the scene of the sinking of the steamship *Djerv*, 12 miles north-northwest of the Skerries, Anglesey, at 6.00 pm and learnt that the survivors had been picked up by another vessel, *HMS PQ63* and landed at Liverpool. *USS Downes* continued her patrol to the northward.

At 9.30 pm when *USS Downes* was south of the Isle of Man, a lookout sighted the conning tower of a submarine close aboard on the port beam disappearing below the surface as soon as she was sighted. *USS Downes* went full speed ahead, circled and dropped two depth charges and then continued her search. At the same time a lookout thought that he had seen a torpedo pass ahead of the ship but this report was unsubstantiated.

**Above:** *USS Downes.*

## Paper Sources

The National Archives of the UK (TNA): Public Record Office (PRO) ADM 137/1514

**Location**
54 20.000 N
04 50.000 W

8 miles northwest of Peel

**Vessel**
Wooden auxiliary motor fishing
boat (a "nobby")
Peel
ON 67,871
9 tons gross, 4 tons net
1917 by Watterson and Neakle,
Peel (note: her official number
gives an original construction
date of 1879)
James Watterson, Peel
36.0 ft x 12.0 ft x 5.3 ft
11.0 m x 3.7 m x 1.6 m

17.30 hours
23rd February 1918

# Attack on the fishing vessel *Girl Emily*

The *Girl Emily*, under John Hughes, skipper, departed Peel on Saturday 23rd February 1918 bound for the fishing grounds to engage in long lining for cod. By 3.30 pm she had finished hauling her long lines and was returning to port shooting her newly baited lines as she went. At about 5.30 pm, when the *Girl Emily* was 8 miles northwest of Peel, skipper Hughes sighted what turned out to be a German submarine about 2 miles away from his vessel coming towards him. The submarine came within 20 yards of the *Girl Emily* and asked if she was engaged in fishing, to which skipper Hughes replied *"Yes"*.

The submarine circled around the *Girl Emily* and then suddenly fired a shot at the defenceless fishing vessel hitting her on the bulwarks aft. Splinters from the shot hit skipper Hughes in the face. Three more shots were fired, two at the bulwarks and one through the sail. The submarine went back alongside the *Girl Emily* and asked for a rope which skipper Hughes supplied. The submarine then towed the *Girl Emily* along and demanded all her catch, valued at 12 pounds sterling, to be transferred over to the submarine. The catch was then paid for but in paper German marks! After the fish was transferred to the submarine, the rope was cast off and the submarine motored away allowing the *Girl Emily* to proceed back to Peel.

The other two crewmen on the *Girl Emily* were the brother of the skipper, James Hughes and the skipper's son, John Hughes. James Hughes was one of the crew of the Peel Lifeboat, *John Monk*, when she made her memorable rescue of 23 lives from the wreck of the Norwegian barque *St George* on 7th October 1889 near Peel.

**Paper Sources**

British Vessels Lost at Sea 1914-1918 and 1939-1945, HMSO

Mona's Herald Tuesday 25.08.1931. Manx National Heritage

Peel City Guardian Saturday 15.10.1938. Manx National Heritage

Peel Shipping Register 1864-93 folio 60, Manx National Heritage

Ramsey Courier Friday 30.08.1935. and 22.01.1937. Manx National Heritage

The National Archives of the UK (TNA): Public Record Office (PRO) ADM137/1514

**Location**
53 51.196 N
04 46.960 W

14 miles southwest by south
(magnetic) of the Calf of Man

**Vessel**
Steel steamship
Christiana (Oslo)
1,458 tons gross
1910 by Nylands Verksted,
Christiana
Triple-expansion engine,
152 nhp, Nylands Verksted,
Christiana
Thor Thoresen, Jr. A/S,
Christiana
254.2 ft x 39.2 ft x 16.5 ft
77.6 m x 12.0 m x 5.0 m

16.00 hours
24th February 1918

# Sinking of the steamship *Sarpfos*

The Norwegian steamship *Sarpfos*, under Hans Johannssan, master, left Swansea on Saturday 23rd February 1918 at 4.00 pm bound for Oddo, Norway calling in at Stornoway for orders, and had on board 2,200 tons of coal. The route instructions had been received from the Shipping Intelligence Officer at Swansea and were followed to the letter.

The South Stack, Anglesey was passed at noon on Sunday 24th February at a distance of 3 miles and the course was shaped to north ½ east (magnetic) for the next position west of the Calf of Man, her speed being 8¾ knots. The weather at the time was fine but hazy, the sea moderate, the wind a fresh northwesterly and visibility about 5 or 6 miles. The second mate was in charge on the bridge and there was a lookout on the forecastle head.

At 4.00 pm when the *Sarpfos* was in a position reported as being about 14 miles southwest by south (magnetic) from the Calf of Man, 53 50 N, 04 47 W, the wake of a torpedo was seen on her portside, close alongside, the torpedo striking the vessel about 2 feet below the waterline at the bulkhead between the engine room and stokehold. Both the engine room and stokehold were completely wrecked. The donkeyman who was on watch in the engine room and a fireman in the stokehold were both killed by the explosion. The port lifeboat was also blown to pieces.

The *Sarpfos* began to settle rapidly. The starboard lifeboat was at once lowered and the remaining crew of eighteen men and one passenger left the ship at once. In a very few minutes the ship had settled down to the level of her upper deck and remained in this position.

Shortly after leaving the ship the periscope of the German submarine *U-105*, under Kapitänleutnant Friedrich Strackerjan, appeared astern of the ship but only remained above the surface for a very short time as if to see what had happened and then moved off to the westward. The crew returned to the *Sarpfos* with the intention of launching the motorboat, but on getting alongside there was the sound like the shot of a gun so the crew pulled back from the ship and waited.

An hour later, the sailing ketch *Howard*, of Kirkwall, approached and took the crew of the *Sarpfos* on board, but would not wait to see if any attempt could be made to save the *Sarpfos*. The *Howard* crowded on all sail and the last the crew of the *Sarpfos* saw of their vessel as darkness fell at 5.10 pm was her bow just above the water. The crew were landed at Liverpool at about 3.00 am on Monday 25th February.

**Wreck Site**
Latitude 53 51.196 N, Longitude 04 46.960 W.

The possible wreck of the *Sarpfos* lies in 90 metres of water. The length of wreck is 48 metres, width 7 metres and height 8 metres. It is orientated 050/230 degrees. The wreck is intact and upright with the bow broken away.

**Paper Sources**
Dictionary of Disasters at Sea during the Age of Steam, Hocking
Lloyd's Register 1918
Lloyd's Wars Losses, the First World War, Casualties to Shipping through Enemy Causes 1914-1918
The National Archives of the UK (TNA): Public Record Office (PRO) ADM 137/1514 and ADM137/3914
World Ship Society

**Location**
53 47.945 N
05 09.849 W

10 miles southwest of the
Calf of Man

**Vessel**
Steel steamship
London
ON 132,624
2,420 tons gross, 1,492 tons net
1910 by R Thomson and Sons
Limited, Sunderland
Triple-expansion engine,
274 nhp, North East Marine
Engineering Company Limited,
Sunderland
William France Fenwick
Company Limited, London
298.0 ft x 42.5 ft x 18.4 ft
90.9 m x 13.0 m x 5.6 m

16.30 hours
26th February 1918

# Sinking of the steamship *Dalewood*

On Tuesday 26th February 1918, the *Dalewood*, under Captain Jones, master, while acting as an Admiralty collier, was bound from Cardiff for Scapa Flow, with 3,300 tons of coal shipped by Mathew and Sons, of Cardiff. At 4.30 pm, when the steamer had run a distance of 35 miles from the South Stack, Anglesey and was estimated to be 10 miles southwest of the Isle of Man (in fact she was 19 miles off the Calf of Man), the master was talking to the first mate, John Page, on the bridge, when the first mate observed the wash of a torpedo coming towards the ship. The torpedo had been fired by the German submarine *U-105*, under Kapitänleutnant Friedrich Strackerjan, and it struck the *Dalewood* on the starboard side of her boiler room. The explosion ripped apart the starboard lifeboat.

The port lifeboat was lowered and eighteen of the crew, who had survived the initial explosion, clambered into it. However, as they did so the steamer foundered, pulling the lifeboat down with it, drowning eleven men. The seven men who survived clung to the upturned lifeboat until *U-105* arrived on the scene and its crew assisted them in righting the lifeboat. The *U-105's* crew showed further compassion by giving the *Dalewood's* survivors some bread and two bottles of rum, before directing them towards the Isle of Man.

At 4.00 am the following day, one of the men in the lifeboat died leaving only six men to land below Hango Hill near Castletown 2 hours later.

The nineteen men who lost their lives were:

AHMAD, fireman
ASKARI, Said, fireman
ASKEW, John Amos, able seaman
BONWICK, George James, third engineer
BROWN, John E, private, RMLI 13676 (Po)
FAIRMANIER, Edwin A, lance corporal, RMLI 12674 (Po)
HASSAN, A, able seaman
HODGSON, Richard, first mate
JONES, David, captain
LEE, William Edward, able seaman
MUHAMMAD, Ali, donkeyman
MUHAMMAD, Hussain, fireman and trimmer
NABI, Abdul, fireman
NASBET, Thomas, second engineer
RIDDLE, William George, second mate
SAID, S, fireman
SALEH, Ali, fireman
TAMURA, T, able seaman
TELFORD, Thomas Butterwicke, steward


## Wreck Site

Latitude 53 47.945 N, Longitude 05 09.849 W

The confirmed wreck of the *Dalewood* lies in 66 metres of water. The length of wreck is 100 metres, width 14 metres and height 8 metres. The wreck is orientated 022/202 degrees and is intact and upright.


## Paper Sources

British Merchant Ships Sunk By U-Boats in the 1914-1918 War, Tennent
British Vessels Lost at Sea 1914-1918 and 1939-1945, HMSO
Dictionary of Disasters at Sea during the Age of Steam, Hocking
Inquest File Index Number 13, Manx National Heritage
Lloyd's Register 1918
Lloyd's Wars Losses, the First World War, Casualties to Shipping through Enemy Causes 1914-1918
The National Archives of the UK (TNA): Public Record Office (PRO) ADM 137/1514 and ADM137/2963
World Ship Society


## Internet Sources

Commonwealth War Graves Commission - www.cwgc.org

17.15 hours
27th February 1918

**Vessel**
Steel steamship
Newcastle
ON 129,750
1,764 tons gross, 1,026 tons net
1910 by S P Austin and Son
Limited, Sunderland
Triple-expansion engine, 193
nhp, George Clark Limited,
Sunderland
Pelton Steamship Company
Limited, Newcastle
265.0 ft x 38.1 ft x 18.5 ft
80.8 m x 11.6 m x 5.6 m

# Sinking of the steamship *Largo*

At 5.15 pm on Wednesday 27th February 1918, while acting as an Admiralty collier transporting 2,400 tons of coal from Barry to Scapa Flow, the *Largo*, under Captain William Horsburgh, master, was zigzagging at a speed of 9 knots and on a heading of north by east ¾ east (magnetic) when a torpedo struck the port side of her number three hold about 14 feet below the waterline. The master had just left the bridge to get a cup of tea when the torpedo struck. The force of the explosion sheared the propeller shaft and the engines raced badly before stopping. The *Largo* settled by the aft end and sank in 10 minutes. Fortunately all the crew of 21 men escaped uninjured and left the *Largo* in the lifeboat.

The German submarine *U-105*, under Kapitänleutnant Friedrich Strackerjan, approached the small boat and a young officer in uniform asked for the name of the ship, where bound and what cargo. One of the men replied *"Largo, bound for Belfast, cargo coal"*. It was not known what rank the officer held but he spoke fairly good English. After receiving the reply to his questions he shouted *"Remember me to Lloyd George"*.

As the wind was a strong west-northwest breeze the crew found it easiest to land at Langness which they did so at 10.30 pm and made their way to the lighthouse where they received refreshments and dry clothes from the keepers. They were later conveyed to Castletown. The master gave the position of sinking as 10 or 12 minutes west of the Calf of Man, or approximately 53 59 N 05 09 W.

The *Largo* had been attacked twice before during the war. On 9th Saturday June 1917, she was chased by a submarine off the north coast of Scotland, but escaped by the use of making smoke. Later on Friday 22nd February 1918, she survived an attempt by a submarine to torpedo her during a passage along the English Channel.

## Wreck Site

Latitude 54 04.660 N, Longitude 05 07.450 W

The probable wreck of the *Largo* lies in 94 metres of water. The length of wreck is 50 metres, width 9 metres and height 6 metres. The wreck is orientated 045/225 degrees and lies on its side.

## Paper Sources

British Merchant Ships Sunk By U-Boats in the 1914-1918 War, Tennent
British Vessels Lost at Sea 1914-1918 and 1939-1945, HMSO
Lloyd's Wars Losses, the First World War, Casualties to Shipping through Enemy Causes 1914-1918
Shipwreck Return Book - Langness Lighthouse (1881 - 1995) Manx National Heritage
The National Archives of the UK (TNA): Public Record Office (PRO) ADM 137/1514
World Ship Society

**Location**
53 55.341 N
04 55.264 W

10 miles southwest by west
of the Calf of Man

**Vessel**
Steel steamship
London
ON 99,099
2,583 tons gross, 1,617 tons net
1892 by J Blumer and Company,
Sunderland
Triple-expansion engine,
249 nhp, North East Marine
Engineering Limited,
Sunderland
Page Shipping Company Limited
(John I Jacobs and Company
Limited, London, manager)
– on charter to the British
Government
305.9 ft x 41.1 ft x 18.8 ft
93.3 m x 12.5 m x 5.7 m
Ex Clan Macrae
Ex Shatt-El-Arab

05.20 hours
2nd March 1918

# Sinking of the steamship *Carmelite*

The *Carmelite,* under Captain Joseph Thomas Francis, master, departed Bilbao, in Spain, on Thursday 21st February 1918 bound for Glasgow, with a cargo of 3,300 tons of iron ore. She called at Milford Haven on Friday 1st March 1918 in order to receive instructions for the final leg of her journey through the Irish Sea. She was to zigzag north and pass within 7 miles of the Calf of Man off the southwest tip of the Isle of Man.

At 5.20 am on Saturday 2nd March, in a fresh northeast wind and bright moonlit night, the *Carmelite* was 10 miles southwest by west of the Calf of Man on a course of north ½ east proceeding at 8 ½ knots when she was torpedoed by the German submarine *U-105*, under Kapitänleutnant Friedrich Strackerjan. The torpedo struck on the starboard side level with the engine room and boiler room bulkhead. The second engineer, Neil McCrae and a fireman, John Turner, were both instantly killed by the explosion of the torpedo. The forepart of the starboard lifeboat was blown away in the explosion. The 27 survivors escaped in the port lifeboat.

The master was the last to leave and was preparing to get into the port jolly boat when he heard cries emanating from the stoke-hole. He went back and found an injured porter jammed in the ventilator hoist. He lowered the hoist and pulled the porter up onto the deck. By this time the after well deck had 2 feet of water on it. The master cut away the after fall of the starboard boat and told the porter to jump in the water, but he refused so the master physically threw him overboard and then jumped into what remained of the boat and pulled the porter into the boat as well. Shortly afterwards, they were both rescued by the crewmen in the port lifeboat.

The *Carmelite* disappeared beneath the waves within 8 minutes of the torpedo striking her. The survivors were subsequently picked up by the steamship *Pearlmoor* at 7.30 am and were then transferred to a Royal Naval patrol vessel which landed them at Holyhead.

The master, Captain Joseph Thomas Francis, of Bank House, Nenas Cross, Pembrokeshire, was awarded £100 by the Board of Trade for his bravery in saving the porter and his name put forward for an Albert medal.

Both Captain Francis and the master of another steamship in the area, the *Idsa*, gave the position of loss of the *Carmelite* as 10 miles southwest of the Calf of Man. The Royal Navy located a wreck in 1945 whilst hunting U-Boats in position 53 55.200 N, 04 56.200 W which was undoubtedly the wreck of *Carmelite.*

## Wreck Site
Latitude 53 55.341 N, Longitude 04 55.264 W

The confirmed wreck of the *Carmelite* lies in 75 metres of water. The length of wreck is 120 metres, width 15 metres and height 9 metres. The wreck is orientated 065/245 degrees and is intact.

## Paper Sources
British Merchant Vessels Sunk by U-Boats in the 1914-1918 War, Tennent
British Vessels Lost at Sea 1914-1918 and 1939-1945, HMSO
Lloyd's Register 1918
Lloyd's Wars Losses, the First World War, Casualties to Shipping through Enemy Causes 1914-1918
The National Archives of the UK (TNA): Public Record Office (PRO) ADM 137/1515 and ADM 137/2964
World Ship Society

## Internet Sources
Commonwealth War Graves Commission - www.cwgc.org

**Location**
54 23.000 N
04 55.000 W

12 miles north-northwest
of Peel

**Vessel**
Wooden motor ketch
Castletown
ON 44,430
60 tons gross, 44 tons net
1862 by T Boyd, Castletown
Rebuilt in 1910
Auxiliary motor, 26 nhp
Joseph Qualtrough, Castletown
69.8 ft x 18.2 ft x 8.5 ft
21.3 m x 5.5 m x 2.6 m

18.30 hours
2nd March 1918

# Sinking of the motor ketch *Bessy*

The *Bessy*, under Evan Quirk, master, left Douglas on Wednesday 26th December 1917 bound for Glasgow with a cargo of 95 tons of scrap iron shipped by Reynolds of Douglas and consigned to A D Kidston, 93 George Street, Glasgow. She tried to round the Point of Ayre, but the wind and tide were against her so she decided to sail down the east coast of the Isle of Man to Port St Mary. Here she remained until Saturday 2nd March 1918 when she set sail for Belfast at high water at 1.00 pm.

At 6.30 pm when she was 12 miles north-northwest of Peel in a choppy sea with a moderate easterly breeze, the master sighted two vessels which he took to be patrol vessels about 3 miles west-northwest of his vessel. The *Bessy* then put reef in her mizzen sail, but immediately the two vessels opened fire on her. The *Bessy's* master brought her round and dropped peak of mainmast and stopped the motor. He ordered the small boat out as shells dropped around them. It was by now evident that the two vessels were German submarines who may well have thought that the *Bessy* was one of Commander Campbell's *"mystery ships"* - armed vessels disguised as merchant men, which lured unwary submarines close to them before revealing their true purpose.

The *Bessy's* crew pulled away in the small boat to get out of the range of the German guns. As they were doing this one shot took away the foremast followed quickly by another, which took down the mainmast. The submarines, which were *U-91*, under Kapitänleutnant Alfred von Glasenapp, and *U-105*, under Kapitänleutnant Friedrich Strackerjan, came to within half a mile of the *Bessy* and finally *U-91* fired a shell that penetrated the fuel tank for the motor and black smoke bellowed from the wrecked ketch. The crew then lost sight of the *Bessy* in the growing darkness and she is assumed to have sunk shortly afterwards. The three crewmen landed at Peel at 4.00 am the following morning.

**Above:** Motor ketch *Bessy* in her earlier days. (Courtesy of Manx National Heritage)

## Wreck Site
Latitude 54 23.000 N, Longitude 04 55.000 W

The wreck of the *Bessy* has not been located.


## Paper Sources
British Vessels Lost at Sea 1914-1918 and 1939-1945, HMSO
Castletown Shipping Register 1847-63 folio 146, Manx National Heritage
Isle of Man Examiner 10.02.1978. Manx National Heritage
Lloyd's Wars Losses, the First World War, Casualties to Shipping through Enemy Causes 1914-1918
Mercantile Navy List 1918
The National Archives of the UK (TNA): Public Record Office (PRO) ADM 137/1515 and ADM 137/2964
World Ship Society


## Internet Sources
Commonwealth War Graves Commission - www.cwgc.org

**Location**
53 40.096 N
05 06.099 W

25 miles northwest (magnetic)
of the Skerries, Anglesey

**Vessel**
Steel steamship
Cork
ON 121,275
1,330 tons gross, 565 tons net
1895 by Wigham Richardson
and Company, Wallsend
Triple-expansion engine, 437
nhp, Wigham Richardson and
Company, Wallsend
City of Cork Steam Packet
Company Limited, Cork
264.5 ft x 35.6 ft x 16.9 ft
80.6 m x 10.9 m x 5.2 m

19.00 hours
2nd March 1918

# Sinking of the steamship *Kenmare*

During World War One the *Kenmare* was attacked by German submarines on four occasions. On Wednesday 27th June 1915 she was attacked by gunfire, when she was off Youghal, Ireland, but she outpaced her attacker and suffered little damage. On Sunday 21st October 1917 a submarine fired a torpedo at her when she was off Holyhead, bound from Liverpool to Cork. The torpedo passed a few feet astern of her, right under her log line. The next attack was on Wednesday 7th November 1917, when she was chased by a submarine, and fired at it to save herself. The final encounter proved fatal.

At 7.00 pm on Saturday evening 2nd March 1918, whilst on a voyage from Liverpool to Cork, the *Kenmare,* under Captain Peter Blacklock, master, was torpedoed, without warning, by the German submarine *U-104*, under Kapitänleutnant Kurt Bernis, when in a position about 25 miles northwest (magnetic) from the Skerries, Anglesey which is about 24 miles southwest of the Calf of Man. Many of the men were in their bunks at the time, and were wakened by the loud explosion, which almost shattered the vessel. The *Kenmare* appeared to have been struck amidships and was to sink within 1 minute of the explosion occurring.

At the time of the explosion Tim O'Brien was in his bunk in the steerage above the propeller and was thrown some yards by the force of the explosion. The lights went out immediately. Four other firemen were sleeping in the same room. There was some confusion in the darkness, but he succeeded in getting a flash lamp and his lifebelt and made for the deck. When he got on deck the ship was sinking fast. Along with William Evans he got into one of the lifeboats and floated off the ship. As they were leaving the ship they grabbed donkeyman, James Barry, and pulled him into the boat. At this time the captain was on deck shouting instructions to the crewmen who were lowering another lifeboat. After leaving the sinking ship they rescued the carpenter, Arthur Phillips, and a gunner, Joseph Brougham, from the water.

Meanwhile, 25 of the crew had put off in the second lifeboat, which upturned, and from which only one man, the chief steward, James Wright, was rescued by the first lifeboat. They found him with his head through the bottom of the boat and extricated him only with great difficulty; Wright was powerless to assist, as one of his arms was broken. They remained in the vicinity for a quarter of an hour in the hope of picking up other men. For about 10 minutes cries were coming from the water for assistance, but owing to the wreckage, they were unable to get to their drowning comrades. At about 7.00 am the following morning the six survivors, out of a total crew of 35, were picked up by the small steam coaster *Glenside* and landed at Dublin. They were then nearly dead with the cold, the majority being only half clad.

Once on the safety of dry land four of the survivors were able to give accounts of their experiences.

James Wright, chief steward, who had sustained a fractured arm, and was badly bruised about the left eye, told how he was talking to Captain Blacklock in the latter's cabin just before the vessel was struck by the torpedo. It was just twilight and nobody saw the submarine. A terrific explosion was the first they knew of anything happening. The *Kenmare* immediately took a big list and commenced to go down by the stern. In a minute and a half or 2 minutes at the most she had disappeared and he was left struggling in the water. When he and the captain realised what was happening they both rushed out on the deck and lowered one of the boats. He, and as many of the others as could, got into the boat, which was upturned by the suction of the vessel foundering and they were all thrown into the sea. *"I was struck by something",* he said, *"as we were thrown out, and knew I was badly hurt, but was thinking of saving myself. I thought of my wife and child, and then made a struggle for it. It was a case of fight for your life. I was swimming about with my arm broken, fighting away for all I was worth for what seemed a long time, but what was probably about 10 minutes, before I was pulled into a boat."* James Wright believed that if he had not been a strong swimmer in his younger days he would never have escaped. He was on the *Kenmare* when she was successful in eluding the German submarine in 1915 when she had no gun, and only escaped by the speed and skill with which the vessel was handled.

Joseph Brougham said the force of the explosion lifted the gun from its socket. The latter struck him on the back, and he was thrown into the sea. He swam about and eventually got hold of some wreckage before being pulled into the lifeboat.

Arthur Phillips, the carpenter, who suffered shock from his experience, said that when the vessel was struck by the torpedo he was in his room. Immediately he went on deck, put on his lifebelt and with others on deck he attempted to launch the lifeboat. *"of course we could not do it"* he proceeded, *"because everything was fast, and the axe and hatchets had been carried away. The vessel was sinking at the time, and a rope was made fast so that we might lower ourselves, but before we could get away the boat sank and I went down with her. Owing to the belt I came up again, and fortunately was clear of the wreckage which was strewn around. I then got on a capsized lifeboat, and all round I could see sailors clinging to wreckage. There was a gig aft, and the donkeyman and fireman got into it. This small boat was astern, having floated off, and after swimming some distance, I was also taken on it. It kept clear of the wreckage and capsized boats. All the other boats were smashed or capsized. Mr Evans was in the gig and if that was not kept right we would have all been lost."*

James Barry, the donkeyman, 72 years of age, had been on the ship for over 22 years, having joined her when she was built. *"It was Mr Evans who saved me,"* he observed. *"I ran up the ladder like a monkey up a stick after hearing the explosion which was a terror out and out. It took the whole ship, and the gun jumped off with the force of the blow. I had not any lifebelt on me at all, nor had I any boots or covering on my head. Owing to the cold I feel now as if I have no feet, and is it any wonder after being exposed as I was for 13 hours?"*

Those saved were:

BARRY, James, donkeyman, 102 Lower Road, Cork
BROUGHAM, Joseph, gunner
EVANS, William, mate, Tayn Boyn, Newquay, Cardigan
O'BRIEN, Tim, fireman, 8 Green Lane, Blackpool, Cork
PHILLIPS, Arthur, carpenter, 33 Hood Lane, Liverpool
WRIGHT, James, steward, 13 Springmount Place, Dillon's Cross, Cork

Those who lost their lives were:

AHERN, Michael, fireman, 7 Glen View, Dillon's Cross, Cork
ASTON, Albert E, gunner, RNVR Bristol Z/3683
BLACKLOCK, Peter, master, 9 Park View, Victoria Road, Cork
BOWEN, Stephen, quartermaster, 4 Harrington Row, Cork
COLEMAN, Michael, fireman, Great William O'Brien Street, Cork
CORCORAN, Patrick John, greaser, 3 Clahane Cottages, Lower Road, Cork
DELEA, Michael, able seaman, 61 Dominick Street, Cork
FENNESSAY, Patrick, able seaman, 51 Hibernian Buildings, Cork

FITZGERALD, James, trimmer, 274 Old Youghal Road, Cork

GOOD, John Jeremiah, able seaman, 8 Fort Street, Cork

GRANT, Geoffrey Joseph, quartermaster, 8 Victoria Road, Cork

HARTNETT, W, cattleman, 56 Watercourse Road, Cork

JOHNSTONE, R, second mate, 1 Grattan Hill, Cork

KEEFE, John, able seaman, Ballinure, Blackrock, Cork

KEENAN, John, greaser, 138 Barrackton, Cork

KEMP, Oscar, cook, 9 Boreenmana Road, Cork

LYONS, William, fireman, 18 Dillon's Cross, St Lukes, Cork

McCARTIE, Percival Hammond, able seaman, Langford Place, Cork

McLOUGHLIN, Robert, fireman, Vennel Street, Glenarm, Co Antrim

McNAMARA, E, cattleman, Walsh's Avenue, Blackpool, Cork

MacAULAY, John, gunner, RNR SD/4315

MOORE, William, able seaman, 7 Corporation Buildings, Cork

MURPHY, Thomas, first engineer, 37 Oriel, Bootle, Liverpool

O'DRISCOLL, Michael John, fireman, 24 Tower Street, Cork

OGLE, Thomas Hugh, second engineer, 10 Kenilworth Street, Bootle, Liverpool

SHAW, Alan C, third engineer, 36 Woodbine Road, Tartown, Huddersfield

SULLIVAN, D, cattleman, Spring Lane, Blackpool, Cork


## Wreck Site

Latitude 53 40.096 N, Longitude 05 06.099 W

The confirmed wreck of the *Kenmare* lies in 64 metres of water. The length of wreck is 70 metres and it is orientated 140/320 degrees.


## Paper Sources

British Merchant Ships sunk by U-Boats in the 1914-1918 War, Tennent

British Vessels Lost at Sea 1914-1918 and 1939-1945, HMSO

Cork Examiner Thursday 07.03.1918

Dictionary of Disasters at Sea during the Age of Steam, Hocking

Isle of Man Weekly Times Tuesday 09.03.1918. Manx National Heritage

Lloyd's Register 1918

Lloyd's Wars Losses, the First World War, Casualties to Shipping through Enemy Causes 1914-1918

The Irish Boats Volume 2: Liverpool to Cork and Waterford, McRonald

The National Archives of the UK (TNA): Public Record Office (PRO) ADM137/2964

World Ship Society


## Internet Sources

Commonwealth War Graves Commission - www.cwgc.org

**Location**
54 22.357 N
04 52.069 W

10 miles south of the Mull
of Galloway

**Vessel**
Iron steamship
Hull
ON 82,494
1,730 tons gross, 982 tons net
1881 by Earl's Company
Limited, Hull
Compound engine, 333 nhp
Ellerman's Wilson Line Limited,
Hull
275.0 ft x 34.6 ft x 19.9 ft
83.8 m x 10.5 m x 6.1 m

02.40 hours
3rd March 1918

# Sinking of the steamship *Romeo*

The *Romeo*, under Captain James Neale, master, left Scapa Flow on Saturday 23rd February 1918 bound for Liverpool. She was on Admiralty charter for carrying meat and provisions to the Fleet, but was returning to Liverpool in ballast after having called in at Stornoway, remaining there for 6 days. She was equipped with a 12-pound gun for defence against enemy submarines.

On Sunday 3rd March 1918 at 2.40 am, she was reportedly about 10 miles south of the Mull of Galloway (in fact she was 11 miles northwest of Peel), steaming at 10 knots and zigzagging. The weather was fine with occasional snow showers, the wind light and the sea smooth. The first officer was in charge on the bridge. There was a lookout on the forecastle head, another on the bridge and one on the gunner's aft platform. All lights on the ship were carefully screened and no navigation lights were burning.

Suddenly, a green and red light appeared off her port bow. Fearful of a collision with another ship, the order was given to show the *Romeo's* navigation lights at her bow. This was a fateful mistake as she had been tricked by German submarine *U-102*, under Kapitänleutnant Curt Beitzen, into giving away her exact position. Within a couple of minutes a torpedo slammed into the *Romeo's* port side between the stoke-hole and engine room. The explosion was terrific and split the ship in half. At first she took a list to port, and then righted herself, before sinking like a stone in less than 2 minutes following the explosion. There was no time for the crew to launch any of the lifeboats and the crew of 32 men was thrown into the water.

The two gun crew, John Compagnon and William Camomile, managed to cling to a swamped boat and eventually bailed it out. Shortly afterwards, they spotted a sailor in the water and hauled him out in to the lifeboat, but he later died at about 10.00 am. At daylight the two gunners managed to get the mast and sail up before being picked up by the steamship *Ardgarvel* at 11.00 am and were later landed at Greenock.

The only other survivor from the *Romeo* was the wireless operator, Arthur Seddon. He was picked up by a trawler and landed at Holyhead by the patrol boat *Kilgobnet* at 11.00 am on Monday 4th March.

The crewmen lost on the *Romeo* were:

ALLEN, Joseph, trimmer
ANDERSON, Herbert, assistant cook
BARGEWELL, George, ship's steward, RN 130104 (Dev)
BIRKINSHAW, Ronald, signalman, RNVR, London Z/2317
BLAIR, George, third engineer
CARNEY, Arthur, fireman
CARR, John, fireman
CROWTHER, Charles, assistant steward
DEADMAN, Robert Methven, wireless operator
FROMM, Thoedore Howard, ship's cook
GUSTAFSON, Hugo, carpenter
HARVEY, Joseph, able seaman
HELM, Richard James, able seaman
HINES, Thomas, fireman and trimmer
KEARNEY, James, fireman
LEE, Martin, seaman
LINACRE, John Edward, boatswain
LONGLEY, John Blyth, second engineer
McLOUGHLIN, David, donkeyman
MIDDLETON, John William, mess room steward
MOLLOY, Patrick, able seaman
NEALE, James, master
NUGENT, Jas Alfred, chief engineer
O'BRIEN, Andrew, fireman and trimmer
O'GORMAN, Thomas Christopher, able seaman
PARRY, John, fireman
PITTS, Albert, chief officer
WHITE, William, able seaman
WILLIAMS, Bertram Percy, steward

**Above:** *SS Romeo.*

## Wreck Site

Latitude 54 22.357 N, Longitude 04 52.069 W

The confirmed wreck of the *Romeo* lies in 46 metres of water (the bell was recovered in the 1990s). The length of wreck is 150 metres, width 20 metres and height 8 metres. The wreck lies in two sections with about 10 metres separating them. The split is aft of the centrally located boilers. It is a large wreck with the bow section lying on its side and quite broken up.

## Paper Sources

British Merchant Ships sunk by U-Boats in the 1914-1918 War, Tennant
British Vessels Lost at Sea 1914-1918 and 1939-1945, HMSO
Dictionary of Disasters at Sea during the Age of Steam, Hocking
The National Archives of the UK (TNA): Public Record Office (PRO) ADM 137/1515

## Internet Sources

Commonwealth War Graves Commission - www.cwgc.org

**Location**
53 43.000 N
04 11.000 W

25 miles north ¼ east of
Beaumaris

**Vessel**
Wooden fishing smack
Douglas
10 tons gross
1910 Peel
H and T Curphey, Douglas

# Sinking of the fishing smack *Marguerite*

The *Marguerite*, under Thomas Lee, skipper, left Bangor, North Wales, on Saturday 9th March 1918 at 9.00 am bound for Douglas with fair weather and a light southwesterly breeze. The crew had travelled to Bangor to collect the fishing boat and sail her to Douglas in the Isle of Man. At 5.30 pm on the same day when it was low water, she was proceeding on her course in a fresh northwesterly breeze, when she encountered the German submarine *UC-75*, under Oberleutnant zur See Walter Schmitz, when she was about midway between Anglesey and the Isle of Man.

On seeing the *Marguerite* the submarine began shelling her, taking her to be a decoy, as at the time the smack had no registration number and was carrying all her sail. After a couple of shots the *Marguerite* stayed and made towards the submarine, but still the shelling continued. One of the crewmen, Richard *"Dicky"* Lee, held up a truce signal, but was dismayed to find that the Germans fired a bullet clean through it.

Thomas Lee, meanwhile, ordered all the canvas to be lowered, and as *UC-75* came closer, he held up his hand and the shelling stopped. When the submarine was alongside the smack two German officers boarded her and stripped off some of the sails taking them to the submarine. This was intended to be makeshift bedding for the prisoners. They then placed a bomb on the *Marguerite* and took off the two Lee brothers and the third man named Harold Daugherty. The *Marguerite* foundered 25 miles north ¼ east of Beaumaris, which is about 25 miles southeast of Langness.

*UC-75* submerged and lay on the seabed for several hours before cruising off in search of its next victim. Walter Schmitz asked to see Thomas Lee and proceeded to conduct a lengthy interrogation through the use of an interpreter. When the commander discovered the smack was not being used for military purposes and was from the Isle of Man (home to many thousands of German prisoners of war), he was much more sympathetic to the crew of the *Marguerite*.

When the submarine surfaced again the smack *Wave* was halted and went the same way, by use of a bomb, as the *Marguerite* 10 miles southwest by west of St Bee's Head. This was 23 hours after the *Marguerite* had been sunk. Together, the crews of the *Wave* and the *Marguerite,* seven in number, were bundled into the *Wave*'s small boat, and were set off in the direction of St Bee's Head. The Germans had given the seamen some food and a compass to ease the journey and the unfortunate seamen eventually landed at Whitehaven at 6.00 pm on Sunday 10th March.

**Wreck Site**
Latitude 53 43.000 N, Longitude 04 11.000 W

The wreck of the *Marguerite* has not been located.

**Paper Sources**
Lloyd's Wars Losses, the First World War, Casualties to Shipping through Enemy Causes 1914-1918
Ramsey Courier Friday 11.10.1929. Manx National Heritage
The National Archives of the UK (TNA): Public Record Office (PRO) ADM137/1515

# HMS Michael attacks a German submarine

**H**MS Michael had just rejoined convoy HX24 at 9.03 am on Sunday 10th March 1918 in position 54 25 N, 04 57 W, about 15 miles northwest of Peel, and was in station ahead of the centre of the convoy, when the periscope of a German submarine was sighted by Yeoman of the Signals, distant about 3 cables (about 600 yards) 1 point on the port bow. *HMS Michael* attacked and dropped two Type D depth charges set to explode at 80 feet. *HMS Victorian* also dropped one charge. HM Ships *Michael* and *Badger* remained in the vicinity for 70 minutes and then rejoined the convoy. There was no evidence of damage to the submarine.

**Above:** *HMS Badger.* (Courtesy of the Imperial War Museum)

## Paper Sources

The National Archives of the UK (TNA): Public Record Office (PRO) ADM 137/1515

**Location**
54 22.000 N
03 50.000 W

10 miles southwest by west
of St Bee's Head

**Vessel**
Wooden fishing ketch
Caernarfon
ON 80,245
47 tons gross, 23 tons net
1890 Brixham
N Ward and Son, Fleetwood

14.00 hours
9th March 1918

# Sinking of the fishing ketch *Wave*

The *Wave*, under Charles Miles, skipper, left Whitehaven on Friday 8th March 1918 at 7.00 pm in fine conditions with a light southeasterly wind. She commenced to trawl and by 2.00 pm on Sunday 10th March had about 1 ½ tons of fish in her hold and was soon to stop trawling and land her catch at Fleetwood.

At this moment she was stationary at her gear whilst 10 miles southwest by west of St Bee's Head in a calm sea and a light northwesterly wind. Suddenly there was a shot fired at her which took away all the rails on the stern together with the mizenmast. The crew then realised a German submarine was about 30 yards off. The submarine, which proved to be *UC-75*, under Oberleutnant zur See Walter Schmitz, then laid against the *Wave* whilst the small boat was launched. The crew of the *Wave* were told to board the submarine and two men from the submarine went on board the *Wave*, placed an explosive charge in the cabin and took all the gear, ropes and blocks that they could manage.

The submarine's crew put the crew of the trawler *Marguerite*, who they had held prisoner, in the small boat along with the crew of the *Wave*. Shortly after pulling away from the *Wave* the charge went off and the *Wave* quickly sank. The small boat made for Whitehaven and safely reached there at 6.00 pm on Sunday 10th March.

**Wreck Site**

Latitude 54 22.000 N, Longitude 03 50.000 W

The wreck of the *Wave* has not been located.

**Paper Sources**

British Vessels Lost at Sea 1914-1918 and 1939-1945, HMSO

The National Archives of the UK (TNA): Public Record Office (PRO) ADM 137/1515

**Location**
54 10.007 N
03 51.795 W

18 miles southeast of
Maughold Head

**Vessel**
Wooden fishing smack
Fleetwood (FD147)
ON 97,926
55 tons gross, 24 tons net
1891 Galmpton
MDI Wedum and others,
Fleetwood
69.3 ft x 18.7 ft x 9.1 ft
21.1 m x 5.7 m x 2.8 m

14.45 hours
10th March 1918

# Sinking of the fishing smack *Sunrise*

The fishing trawler *Sunrise*, under William Slinger, skipper, left Fleetwood at 7.00 am on Friday 8th March 1918 just after high water in a light northeasterly wind and fine weather. By Sunday 10th March she had 30 boxes of fish in her hold, and at 2.45 pm, the tide being 4 hours on the ebb, the weather fine with a light southeast wind and a ground swell from the southwest, the *Sunrise* was fishing with a trawl about 18 miles southeast of Maughold Head when the master's attention was called to a German submarine about 300 yards on her starboard side.

*UC-75*, under Oberleutnant zur See Walter Schmitz, was observed to be manoeuvring on the surface and shortly afterwards fired one shot over the vessel doing no damage. The master immediately gave orders to launch the small boat and all four crew escaped safely. However, Walter Schmitz ordered the small boat to pull back to the smack with some of his crew who at once started looting the *Sunrise*. The submarine pulled alongside the smack and the Germans loaded all the *Sunrise*'s provisions, eleven baskets of fresh fish, a clock, the weatherglass, foghorn, ropes and twine onto their vessel.

The *Sunrise*'s crew were then ordered to pull towards the land whilst the *UC-75*'s crew sank the *Sunrise* with bombs. After they had rowed some distance the submarine once more came alongside and the master was ordered to give up his oilskins and what little food they had with them. They were left with only a small loaf of bread and 3 inches of fresh water in a bucket. The submarine's gunner also demanded the ship's compass and the master's sea boots, but Walter Schmitz ordered him not to take them.

**Wreck Site**

Latitude 54 10.007 N, Longitude 03 51.795 W

The possible wreck of the *Sunrise* lies in 22 metres of water. There is an area of debris, 0.5 metres high, which is thought to be a wooden wreck.

**Paper Sources**

British Vessels Lost at Sea 1914-1918 and 1939-1945, HMSO

Lloyd's Wars Losses, the First World War, Casualties to Shipping through Enemy Causes 1914-1918

Ramsey Courier Friday 11.10.1929. Manx National Heritage

The National Archives of the UK (TNA): Public Record Office (PRO) ADM 137/1515

World Ship Society

# Bodies recovered from the steamship *Sea Gull*

On Saturday afternoon 23rd March 1918, Mr J S Gell, Coroner, conducted an inquiry in the Oddfellows Hall, Port St Mary, into the death of a seafarer, whose body had been found by George Woodworth floating in the bay off Gansey at noon the previous day. He and a Mr Royston went out in a boat, and they towed the body in by the lifebelt which the deceased still held in his left hand. There was another lifebelt fastened around the body.

The Coroner, in opening the inquest, remarked that papers found on the body gave the man's name as Vicente Perello, born in 1895 in Denia, Spain. He was employed on the steamship *Sea Gull*, of London, 976 tons gross, which was lost 7 miles northeast of Point Lynas, Anglesey, on Saturday 16th March 1918 while on a voyage from Le Havre to Liverpool with a general cargo. After other evidence was given by Dr Chambers and police sergeant W Faragher, the jury at the inquest gave a verdict of *"found drowned."* The interment took place at Rushen Churchyard the next afternoon, the Reverend William Cannell officiating.

**Above:** *SS Sea Gull.*

The second body to wash ashore from the *Sea Gull* was spotted on rocks below the mines at Langness on Saturday 23rd March 1918. At the inquest the body was identified as that of Alfred Dunthorne, 38 years of age, of 140 Second Avenue, Manor Park, London, a fireman on board the *Sea Gull*. A verdict of *"found drowned"* was given by jury at the inquest held by Mr J S Gell, Coroner, at the Court House, Castletown.

By a strange coincidence the bodies of two brothers, James and Bernard Darragh, sons of James Darragh, of 4 Dombey Street, Liverpool, were both washed ashore on the Manx coast a few days later on Good Friday 1918. They were also members of the crew of the *Sea Gull*. The body of Bernard, who was unmarried, 23 years of age, and a steward on the ill-fated vessel, was found on the beach at Port Erin by Walter Cregeen at 4.00 am on Friday 29th March 1918. The body of James, who was unmarried, 26 years of age, and a fireman, was found by Henry Moore on the Brewery Beach, near the Shore Hotel, Gansey, at 7.00 pm on Saturday 30th March. Both men were fully dressed, and identification papers and photographs were found in their pockets.

At the following inquest, James Darragh, senior, identified the bodies of his two sons and the jury returned a verdict of *"found drowned"* in each case. Coroner LaMothe extended his sincere sympathy to the bereaved father and the other members of his family.

**Paper Sources**
Isle of Man Examiner Saturday 30.03.1918. and 06.04.1918. Manx National Heritage

**Internet Sources**
Commonwealth War Graves Commission - www.cwgc.org

**Location**
54 09.000 N
04 00.000 W

14 miles south of
Maughold Head

**Vessel**
Iron steamship
Belfast
ON 83,926
274 tons gross, 107 tons net
1880 by McIlwaine and Lewis,
Belfast
Compound engine, 50 rhp
McIlwaine and Lewis, Belfast
Cliffmore Steamship Company
Limited (S Stewart and
Company, manager)
157.5 ft x 21.6 ft x 10.8 ft
48.0 m x 6.6 m x 3.3 m
Ex Parkmore

19.40 hours
26th March 1918

# Attack on the steamship *Cliffmore*

T he *Cliffmore*, left Garston on Tuesday 26th March 1918 bound for Belfast, with a cargo of coal. Nothing of importance occurred until the vessel was 14 miles south (magnetic) of Maughold Head, when at 7.40 pm a submarine was observed off the starboard beam distant about 1 mile. The *Cliffmore* was steering north by west (magnetic) and the submarine seemed to be steering a parallel course.

As soon as the submarine spotted the *Cliffmore*, she starboarded her helm and her course altered 16 points, which left her heading south by east (magnetic). The *Cliffmore's* 12-pounder was loaded and the gun's crew stood by, but owing to fading daylight and the fact that the submarine soon submerged after altering course, fire was not opened on the submarine.

**Paper Sources**
Lloyd's Register 1916
The National Archives of the UK (TNA): Public Record Office (PRO) ADM137/1515

**Location**
54 17.000 N
05 09.000 W

14 miles northwest of the
Calf of Man

**Vessel**
Steel steamship
Glasgow
ON 118,569
2,539 tons gross, 1,616 tons net
1905 by Wood, Skinner and
Company Limited, Newcastle
Triple-expansion engine,
266 nhp, North East Marine
Engineering Company Limited,
Newcastle
Donald and Taylor, Glasgow
313.3 ft x 45.0 ft x 20.1 ft
95.5 m x 13.7 m x 6.1 m

01.40 hours
28th March 1918

# Attack on the steamship *Leafield*

The *Leafield,* under Captain William McCone, master, left Bilbao on Thursday 21st March 1918 bound for Glasgow via Penzance laden with a cargo of 4,000 tons of iron ore. At 1.40 am on Thursday 28th March a German submarine was sighted under the bow when the *Leafield* was in position 54 17 N, 05 09 W, about 14 miles northwest of the Calf of Man. It was initially mistaken for rocks inside of the South Rock Light Vessel. The ship's helm was put hard a port which brought the submarine alongside the *Leafield.* The submarine opened fire from astern, firing six rounds, the *Leafield* replying with two rounds from her 12-pound gun. The steamer was hit by shrapnel but did not suffer any direct hits.

This was the fourth time that the *Leafield* had been attacked by an enemy submarine. Captain McCone had been in command on each occasion and received a mention in dispatches for his previous encounter on 3rd December 1917. Following this fourth incident the Mercantile Marine Awards Committee recommended him for a Distinguished Service Cross.

**Above:** *SS Leafield.*

## Paper Sources

Lloyd's Register 1916

The National Archives of the UK (TNA): Public Record Office (PRO) ADM137/1515

**Location**
54 35.448 N
04 24.885 W

10 miles southwest of
Burrow Head, Scotland

**Vessel**
Steel steamship
Liverpool
ON 115,582
3,575 tons gross, 2,261 tons net
1902 by Hall, Russell and
Company Limited, Aberdeen
Triple-expansion engine, 484
nhp, Hall, Russell and Company
Limited, Aberdeen
Charente Steamship Company
Limited, Liverpool (Thomas
and James Harrison, Liverpool,
managers)
350.2 ft x 43.3 ft x 28.0 ft
106.8 m x 13.2 m x 8.5 m

07.18 hours
28th March 1918

# Sinking of the steamship *Inkosi*

The *Inkosi*, under Captain John Arthur, master, left Liverpool at 6.00 pm on Wednesday 27th March 1918 bound for Lamlash and then Pernambuco, Brazil, with a cargo of 2,000 tons of coal and 300 tons of general cargo. At 7.18 am on Thursday 28th March, she was zigzagging at full speed and on a course of N82W (magnetic) when a torpedo suddenly struck the vessel amidships on the port side between the engine room and stoke-hole. At this point she was about 10 miles southwest of Burrow Head in southwest Scotland (about 11 miles north of the Point of Ayre). The explosion stopped the steamer immediately and three firemen on duty were killed. The boats were lowered on Captain Arthur's order, but the foremost boat had been rendered useless by the force of the explosion and in lowering the port after boat, one of the tackles was carried away rendering that boat useless also. The remaining boats were safely lowered and most of the 47 surviving crewmen began to get into the boats.

Meanwhile, the two gunners, Lieutenant Corporal W N Griffiths and Private S A Mahugh, RMLI remained with the gun on the aft platform, ready in case the submarine showed herself on the surface. The captain shouted to the gunners to abandon ship, as he was about to do after he had destroyed the confidential papers. The decks aft were now awash and the engine room was full of water. The remaining men then made their way to the boats, which quickly pulled off to a safe distance.

The *Inkosi* didn't appear to be settling as fast as originally anticipated so Captain Arthur said that he would board her again. The two gunners agreed to go with him and manned the gun ready to fire it in order to attract attention from other ships in the area. Unfortunately, the gun misfired and, as the gunners tried to ready the gun again, Captain Arthur shouted to them to take to the boat immediately. The gunners depressed the gun in case it went off and joined Captain Arthur in the lifeboat again. As they pulled clear a periscope appeared and shortly afterwards the German submarine *U-96*, under Kapitänleutnant Heinrich Jeß, surfaced off the port bow of the steamship to finish off the *Inkosi* with her deck guns.

The *U-96* fired over a dozen rounds at the *Inkosi* and eventually at 8.18 am the steamer sank about 6 miles southwest of Burrow Head. The submarine made no attempt to question the crew of the *Inkosi* who set off in the direction of Burrow Head with the *U-96* still motoring around the spot where the *Inkosi* had gone down.

Both lifeboats landed at the Isle of Whithorn and it was only then that three firemen were discovered to be missing and were presumed to have died in the attack on the steamer. They were:

FRACKLETON, William, fireman and trimmer
HERTFORD, John, fireman and trimmer
ROWAN, Hugh, fireman and trimmer

**Above:** *SS Inkosi.*

## Wreck Site

Latitude 54 35.448 N, Longitude 04 24.885 W

The confirmed wreck of the *Inkosi* lies in 48 metres of water (the bell was recovered in 2004). The length of wreck is 110 metres, width 20 metres and height 16 metres. The wreck is orientated 112/292 degrees and is broken about half way along its length. The two halves lie on slightly different alignments.

**Above:** *The ship's bell from the SS Inkosi.*

## Paper Sources

British Merchant Ships Sunk by U-Boats in the 1914-1918 War, Tennent
British Shipping Fleets, Joseph Fisher and Sons, Fenton and Patterson
British Vessels Lost at Sea 1914-1918 and 1939-1945, HMSO
Lloyd's Wars Losses, the First World War, Casualties to Shipping through Enemy Causes 1914-1918
The National Archives of the UK (TNA): Public Record Office (PRO) ADM 137/1515 and ADM 137/2964

## Internet Sources

Commonwealth War Graves Commission - www.cwgc.org

**Location**
54 01.000 N
05 12.500 W

13 miles west of the
Calf of Man

**Vessel**
Steel steamship
Liverpool
ON 135,574
3,942 tons gross, 2,448 tons net
1914 by Napier and Miller
Limited, Glasgow
Triple-expansion engine, 449
nhp, Dunsmuir and Jackson
Limited, Glasgow
F Leyland and Company
Limited, Liverpool
365.2 ft x 47.8 ft x 27.0 ft
111.3 m x 14.6 m x 8.2 m

00.00 hours
29th March 1918

# Attack on the steamship *Oranian*

The *Oranian*, under Captain William Hannaford, master, departed from Liverpool bound for Lamlash, Isle of Arran on Friday 29th March 1918. Later that day with the Chicken Rock bearing N85E, she was in company with the steamship *Huronian*, when she was attacked by a German submarine. The torpedo passed 40 yards astern of the *Oranian*. After the attack she altered course in the direction from where the torpedo had originated and kept on that course for 20 minutes before altering course for the South Rock, County Down, zigzagging throughout.

**Paper Sources**
Lloyd's Register 1916
The National Archives of the UK (TNA): Public Record Office (PRO) ADM137/1515

Location
53 38.080 N
04 49.435 W

12 miles west by north
of Calf of Man
(position where first attacked)

03.45 hours
31st March 1918

# Sinking of the steamship *Conargo*

**Vessel**
Steel steamship
London
ON 139,005
4,312 tons gross, 2,176 tons net
1902 by Flensburger Schiffshb.
Ges., Flensburg
Triple-expansion engine, 471
nhp, Flensburger Schiffshb.
Ges., Flensburg
Commonwealth of Australia -
Melbourne
375.0 ft x 47.9 ft x 17.0 ft
114.3 m x 14.6 m x 5.2 m
Ex Altona

The *Conargo*, under Captain Ernest Clutterbuck, master, left South East Harrington Dock, Liverpool at 11.00 am on Saturday 30th March 1918 bound for Lamlash Bay, Isle of Arran, in ballast, on Government Service where she would receive further orders. She proceeded out into the River Mersey and anchored with tugs in attendance. The officer in charge of the Otter appliances tested both port and starboard sets during the afternoon to ensure that they worked satisfactorily. At 7.30 pm she left the Mersey with the pilot in charge.

At midnight, Captain Clutterbuck went on deck and found the steamship making a course straight for a position off Point Lynas, which was passed 10 miles off at 00.10 am. The Captain remarked to the pilot, James Mills, that it would be necessary to zigzag. Number three zigzag was immediately put into operation and as an extra precaution was broadened at irregular intervals at periods of every hour. Captain Clutterbuck then noted two trawlers on the starboard bow steering in the opposite direction. He remarked to the pilot that it was strange for trawlers to be showing a green and white deck light only, and considered the absence of a mast head light peculiar. However, the pilot reassured him that it was common for such vessels to be showing low lights only. The Captain accepted the pilot's statement but kept zigzagging and began to get a bit anxious. The fact that at the end of each zigzag the two vessels kept on appearing ahead of the *Conargo* seemed to indicate that something was wrong.

On Sunday 31st March at 3.45 am, the pilot went onto the bridge with orders from Captain Clutterbuck to alter course to N19W which was carried out at once by putting the helm to port by 33 degrees. The steamer was swinging around in a position 12 miles west by north of the Calf of Man when a torpedo hit the ship forward, blowing up the chain locker and firemen's forecastle. The pilot left the bridge and was immediately replaced by the master who ordered the engines to be stopped. The boats were lowered and manned. Captain Clutterbuck gave instructions for a radio message to be broadcast, but the aerial had been carried away in the explosion. However, the wireless operator was sure that he had managed to get out an earlier SOS prior to being given the instruction by Captain Clutterbuck.

The attacking German submarine *U-96*, under Kapitänleutnant Heinrich Jeß, fired a second torpedo at the now stationary and vulnerable *Conargo*. This second torpedo struck the *Conargo* on her port side at 4.20 am in a line with the fore bridge. The explosion also tore apart the lifeboat in charge of the boatswain, which was waiting alongside the steamer, killing all ten men on board. The remaining crew took to the other three boats in a desperate attempt to clear the steamer as the submarine had surfaced off her bow and they were fearful of her opening fire with her deck gun. In their haste, one injured crewman was left behind. However, the attack did not materialise so the 45 survivors out of an original crew of 54 men and the pilot waited for daybreak. By 8.00 am it transpired that one of the boats had broken away from the other two and was heading in a westerly direction for the Irish coast. The two boats remaining by the still floating *Conargo* then split up; one heading in an easterly direction for the Isle of Man, the other not moving far. However, the occupants of both boats, totalling 24 men and the pilot, were picked up by the Italian steamer *Nitor* and landed at Holyhead at 4.50 pm.

Meanwhile, the boat heading for the Irish coast under sail eventually sighted land at 6.00 pm on the starboard bow and shortly afterwards a collier was spotted heading straight for them. She turned out to be the steamship *Marie*, of Arklow, whose master was suspicious of the small boat and kept his gun trained on it until he had established that it was genuinely a shipwrecked crew. The collier turned back to Dublin and landed the survivors, consisting of the master and 19 of the crew, at 9.50 pm.

The *Conargo* had been abandoned by her crew in position 53 59 N, 05 18 W, but contrary to their belief did not sink. It was not until 7.30 am on Monday 1st April, that she was located by the steam trawler *Dunnet* in position 53 42 N 05 07 W and a fire was observed to still be burning in the forecastle. A second trawler *Vanessa II* reported her afloat in position 53 47 N 05 00 W not long afterwards. The Senior Naval Officer at HM Naval Base, Holyhead then dispatched the steam trawlers *Robert Cloughton*, *John Clay*, and *Ben Meide*, together with the motor launches *MLS 219, 221* and *231*, the tug *HS36* and two drifters. In addition a yacht, two steam trawlers and two destroyers were dispatched from Kingstown (now Dun Laoghaire). A motor torpedo boat also arrived on the scene shortly after the *Dunnet* and *Vanessa II*.

The *Vanessa II* and *John Clay* took the *Conargo* in tow whilst the *Robert Cloughton* steered her and the remaining vessels formed a submarine screen around her. Towing operations came to a halt at 7.45 pm when the *Conargo's* anchor worked loose and streamed out effectively anchoring the steamer. The *Vanessa II* sent a boarding party over to her to let go the anchor cable in order to free the vessel. The tow continued and at 9.50 pm the *Dunnet* sighted a submarine about 300 yards off and immediately afterwards a torpedo exploded into the side of the *Conargo*. The *Dunnet* fired two shots at the submarine, put her helm over to follow the submarine's wake and dropped several depth charges, but the attack proved unsuccessful.

The fleet of vessels guarded the *Conargo* all night and kept further look out for the submarine, but the *Conargo* finally foundered at 5.22 am on Tuesday 2nd April between the Isle of Man and Anglesey.

The ten crewmen who lost their lives in the sinking of the *Conargo* were:

ALDWINCKLE, Harry, fireman
DEEGAN, James Clark, fireman
GRUNDY, Andrew, scullion
JACKSON, Patrick, fireman
JORDAN, James, fireman
MALONE, Henry James, donkeyman
MORRIS, S, trimmer
MURPHY, J, trimmer
POWER, Christopher, fireman
POWER, Thomas, boatswain

## Wreck Site
Latitude 53 38.080 N, Longitude 04 49.435 W

The confirmed wreck of the *Conargo* lies in 45 metres of water (the bell was recovered in the 1995). The length of wreck is 115 metres, width 15 metres and height 15 metres. The wreck is orientated 060/240 degrees and is broken into three sections.

**Above:** *SS Conargo when she was named the SS Altona.*

## Paper Sources

British Merchant Ships Sunk by U-Boats in the 1914-1918 War, Tennent

British Vessels Lost at Sea 1914-1918 and 1939-1945, HMSO

Dictionary of Disasters at Sea during the Age of Steam, Hocking

Lloyd's Register 1918

Lloyd's Wars Losses, the First World War, Casualties to Shipping through Enemy Causes 1914-1918

The National Archives of the UK (TNA): Public Record Office (PRO) ADM137/344, ADM137/634, ADM137/1515 and ADM137/2964

World Ship Society

## Internet Sources

Commonwealth War Graves Commission - www.cwgc.org

## Location
54 15.000 N
05 14.000 W

17 miles west of Peel

## Vessel
Steel steamship
Liverpool
ON 106,834
7,323 tons gross, 4,784 tons net
1897 by C S Swan and Hunter
Limited, Newcastle
Triple-expansion engine,
502 nhp, Northeast Marine
Company Limited, Newcastle
Canadian Pacific Railway Ocean
Lines (Canadian Pacific Ocean
Services Limited, Montreal,
manager)
470.0 ft x 56.1 ft x 32.0 ft
143.3 m x 17.1 m x 9.8 m

06.02 hours
31st March 1918

# Attack on the steamship *Milwaukee*

The *Milwaukee*, under Captain John Nathaniel Griffiths, master, departed from Liverpool on 30th March 1918 bound for Lamlash, Isle of Arran with 470 tons of general cargo and a crew of 62 hands. At 6.02 am on Sunday 31st March 1918 she was in position 54 15 N, 05 14 W (about 17 miles west of Peel) when the track of a torpedo was seen heading towards the vessel at a distance of 200 yards. Luckily, the torpedo missed its target and for 20 minutes after the attack the *Milwaukee* altered course on a heading of N70E (magnetic) which was approximately the course of the torpedo and then she altered course for a position off the South Rock, County Down, zigzagging throughout.

## Paper Sources
Lloyd's Register 1916
The National Archives of the UK (TNA): Public Record Office (PRO) ADM137/1515

**Location**
54 03.000 N
05 06.000 W

10 miles west by south
of the Calf of Man

**Vessel**
Steel steamship
Liverpool
ON 113,476
20,904 tons gross, 13,449 tons
net
1901 by Harland and Wolff,
Belfast
Quadruple-expansion engine,
1,524 nhp, Harland and Wolff,
Belfast
Ocean Steam Navigation
Company Limited, James Street,
Liverpool (the White Star Line)
680.9 ft x 75.3 ft x 44.1 ft
207.6 m x 23.0 m x 13.4 m

07.34 hours
31st March 1918

# Attack on the steamship *Celtic*

The *Celtic* departed from Liverpool on Sunday 31st March 1918 bound for New York with a crew of 320 but no passengers. At 7.34 am she was 10 miles west by south of the Calf of Man when she was torpedoed without warning by the German submarine *UB-77*, under Kapitänleutnant Wilhelm Meyer. The torpedo struck on the port side of her boiler room leaving a hole in her hull large enough to drive a wagon through. She took on a heavy list and it was feared that she would capsize and sink at any moment. Her crew, with the exception of six men who were killed in the explosion, took to the ship's boats, while the liner drifted off on her own.

Kapitänleutnant Meyer decided to finish off the *Celtic* and a quarter of an hour later a second torpedo struck her on the starboard side ripping another huge hole in her hull in the bunker hold. However, instead of sending her to the bottom, the second hole allowed her to fill with sea water on the opposite side of the ship to the initial flooding and she righted herself back to an even keel, and her bulkheads did the rest. The lifeboats from Port St Mary and Castletown were called out to assist, but were turned back by a destroyer. The *Celtic* was taken in tow by three Liverpool tugs and several patrol vessels and anchored in Peel Bay in the Isle of Man at 9.00 pm on Monday 1st April.

During the night the Isle of Man Steam Packet Company vessel *Tynwald* took out from

Liverpool at high speed, the divers and necessary equipment for the repair of the *Celtic*. After emergency repairs she was taken to Belfast for full repair. About half the survivors remained with the *Celtic* and the other half were taken to Liverpool by a naval vessel.

**Above:** *SS Celtic.*

The six men who died in the attack on the *Celtic* were:

BODIE, Robert, refrigerator greaser
GLEAVE, William Edwin, trimmer
JEFFERS, Charles, chiefs boots
McDONALD, Stanley Angus, senior fourth engineer
RICHARDSON, George, fireman
ROUTLEDGE, Samuel, fireman

**Paper Sources**
Isle of Man Times Saturday 18.01.1919. Manx National Heritage
Lloyd's Register 1916
Ramsey Courier Friday 16.05.1919. Manx National Heritage
The Isle of Man and the Great War, Sargeaunt
The National Archives of the UK (TNA): Public Record Office (PRO) ADM137/2964

**Internet Sources**
Commonwealth War Graves Commission - www.cwgc.org

**Location**
53 54.000 N
04 00.000 W

22 miles southeast of
Douglas Head

**Vessel**
Wooden steam drifter
Lowestoft (LT61)
ON 135,741
80 tons gross, 40 tons net
1913 by John Chambers, Oulton
Broad
Compound steam engine, Elliot
and Garrood
British Admiralty
82.3 ft x 18.1 ft x 9.2 ft
25.1 m x 5.5 m x 2.8 m

07.05 hours
2nd April 1918

# HMS Dick Whittington attacks a submarine

At 7.05 am on Tuesday 2nd April 1918, *HMD Dick Whittington* was steering south with *HMD Hope* a mile and a half on the port beam, with a convoy of 15 ships proceeding south 4 miles off her port beam. Suddenly, the conning tower of a German submarine was observed on *HMD Dick Whittington's* starboard beam distant about 4,000 yards proceeding south at great speed and leaving quite a wake with her conning tower. *HMD Dick Whittington* altered course and set off at full speed for the submarine, opening fire as she went. She fired six rounds before the submarine submerged. Once over the position in which the submarine had submerged the *HMD Dick Whittington* deployed her hydrophone and ordered the trawler *Hope* to steam 1 mile south of her position and put her hydrophone over. Nothing was heard by either vessel and they patrolled the vicinity, which was 22 miles southeast of Douglas Head, for a further 24 hours, but nothing further was heard of the submarine.

**Paper Sources**
The National Archives of the UK (TNA): Public Record Office (PRO) ADM137/634

**Location**
53 41.000 N
05 15.000 W

25 miles southwest
of the Calf of Man

**Vessel**
Steel P-Class Sloop
694 tons displacement
1913 by Workman Clark and
Company, Belfast
Steam Turbines, 3,500 ihp,
Workman Clark and Company,
Belfast
British Admiralty
247.0 ft x 25.5 ft x 8.0 ft
75.3 m x 7.8 m x 2.4 m

18.20 hours
3rd April 1918

# HMS PC61 attacks a German submarine

A t 6.20 pm on Wednesday 3rd April 1918, with the Calf of Man bearing 15 miles to the northeast, a hostile submarine was sighted on the surface by the Special Service Ship or "Q-ship" HMS PC61, commanded by Frank A Worsley, who had been the captain of explorer Shackleton's ship Endurance before joining the war effort as a Royal Navy Reservist.

The submarine was steering N20W at approximately 15 knots, at a distance of 9 miles from HMS PC61. She increased to full speed heading towards the submarine on a course of S50W. At 6.30 pm the submarine altered course to about S60W and appeared to be running from HMS PC61 at a speed in the region of 19 knots, as HMS PC61 was making 21 knots and only slowly making ground on the submarine.

Fifteen minutes later, the submarine turned 10 to 15 degrees, at a distance of 6 miles from HMS PC61, and dived rapidly in position 53 41 N, 05 15 W. Closing the position where the submarine was last sighted, HMS PC61 dropped five depth charges, all set to 200 feet in an area 3 miles square. One depth charge failed to explode and after examining the chart, Frank Worsley concluded that the depth charge was dropped on an isolated 30 fathom sounding and consequently did not sink to sufficient depth to detonate. A sixth depth charge, set to 150 feet, was then dropped, but no positive results were observed.

HMS PC61 remained in the vicinity until daybreak on Thursday 4th April, but saw no further sign of the submarine.

**Paper Sources**
The National Archives of the UK (TNA): Public Record Office (PRO) ADM 137/1516

**Location**
53 59.000 N
05 00.000 W

7 miles southwest
of the Calf of Man

**Vessel**
Steel steam yacht
ON 123,137
323 tons gross, 111 tons net
1908 by Liffey Dockyard, Dublin
Triple-expansion engines, 140
hp, David Rowan and Company,
Glasgow
British Admiralty
155.0 ft x 24.5 ft x 12.5 ft
47.3 m x 7.5 m x 3.8 m

19.30 hours
4th April 1918

# Possible submarine kill by *HM Yacht Helga*

O n the evening of Thursday 4th April 1918 at 7.30 pm, *HM Yacht Helga*, under
Lieutenant Edward Woodcock, RNR, commanding officer, was on patrol southwest
of the Calf of Man, when a thin well-defined track of oil was observed about half a mile
in length, which appeared to be extending east. Lieutenant Woodcock at once sounded
action, and altered course to run along the oil track, putting engines to utmost speed,
about 13 knots. The end of the track appeared to be extending at good speed, and
when within 400 to 500 yards, a wake of a submarine was observed, then a swirl, and a
periscope appeared for about 8 seconds, then it submerged.

Every endeavour was made to ram the submarine, but it took 3 to 4 minutes to catch it,
its wake being clearly discernible. *HM Yacht Helga* passed over the submarine and when
150 yards ahead, dropped a depth charge and then a second one some 100 yards ahead
of the first depth charge, before circling around. The submarine did not alter course
at once, but immediately after the depth charges exploded, air bubbles, as from three
or four divers, were observed in a position between the two depth charges. In 2 to 3
minutes oil commenced rising in volumes, then making due allowance for the tide, *HM
Yacht Helga* dropped two depth charges together, then placed the trawler *William Butler*,
which had now arrived on the scene, in position and then dropped another depth charge.
Bubbles of air continued to rise, but gradually decreased in quantity until 9.30 pm when
they finally ceased. Dahn buoys were placed at the location.

*HM Yacht Helga* lay over the submarine listening with her hydrophone all night. The
trawlers *William Butler* and *Imelda*, which arrived later, also listened with hydrophones.
No movement from a submarine was heard.

At daybreak on Friday 5th April, oil was still rising thickly from the same spot. The trawler *Imelda* then exploded two single towing charges as deep as possible. *HM Yacht Helga* remained over the submarine, till sweepers arrived at 3.00 pm. Using ground sweeps, they caught what they considered to be a submarine almost at once, but as they could not lift, they slipped the sweep, and *HM Yacht Helga* then dropped four more depth charges. The two sweepers, the *William Butler* and *HM Yacht Helga* remained on position through the night using their hydrophones but no movement was heard.

**Above:** *HM Yacht Helga* during the war.

Early the next morning on Saturday 6th April, oil was still rising faintly. A new supply of depth charges arrived by motor launch. The sweepers again began operations and quickly became fast to a possible submarine, but were unable to raise anything. The sweep then parted and so a buoy was placed on the object and five depth charges were exploded over the site in a star formation. At this point Lieutenant Woodcock felt confident that he had destroyed a German submarine and reported the position of the wreck to be at 53 59 N, 05 00 W.

Had *HM Yacht Helga* destroyed a German submarine? Initially, the Director of Naval Intelligence thought that she had and that it *"was probably of the UC type"* and *"ceased to operate after the attack."*

In order to gain more evidence the Admiralty telegraphed the Commodore at Kingstown (now Dun Laoghaire) on Saturday 20th April ordering a large explosive charge to be carefully placed by means of a sweep wire so as to be in contact with the submarine and some of the wreckage should be sent to the Director of Naval Intelligence. This was done but the first charge that was exploded only brought up a large quantity of heavy oil and petrol. A second charge was more successful on Wednesday 24th April and two candles, a lump of grease, part of a canvas screen and about 18 by 10 feet of wire rails and stanchions were recovered from the wreck. The small articles and a sketch of the rail stanchions were forwarded to the Director of Naval Intelligence.

**Above:** Fishery cruiser *Muirchu*, ex *HM Yacht Helga*, Irish Free State Government.
(Courtesy of the National Maritime Museum)

On the Monday 20th May 1918 the Director of Naval Intelligence office reported that the origin of the canvas and candles could not be traced, but the rail fittings *"do not appear to have come from a submarine."* The case was classified provisionally a *"probable kill."* and an award of £1,000 was awarded to those on board *HM Yacht Helga*. Seven of the crew were decorated or were mentioned in dispatches. Lieutenant Edward Woodcock RNR was awarded the Distinguished Service Cross. Deckhand William Ernest Hebb and leading deckhand Ernest Edwin Duff were awarded the Distinguished Service Medal. Lieutenant Patrick Duane RNR, Engineer Sub-Lieutenant Robert Kearon RNR, Warrant Officer (Second Engineer) Patrick David Starrs and Third Engineer Herbert Moore were mentioned in dispatches.

Did *HM Yacht Helga* destroy a German U-Boat? German naval records do not show any submarines lost on 4th April 1918. Indeed, no German submarines were lost in the North Irish Sea during the entire First World War (with the possible exception of *U-69* in July 1917). It would appear that *HM Yacht Helga* at least initially attacked a submarine but it must have slipped past her and escaped. When the *"kill"* was swept with a wire from a pair of trawlers the objects that were recovered were not typical of a submarine and far more likely to have come from a wreck of a steamship (the author has seen copies of the sketches in the Admiralty records). When the submarine gave *HM Yacht Helga* the slip, by coincidence there must have been an existing wreck at the location and it was this wreck that *HM Yacht Helga* thought was the submarine lying paralysed on the seabed.

Which wreck was it? The nearest wreck to the reported position of the incident (53 59 N, 05 00 W) is that of the steamship *Downshire* lost 3 years earlier in February 1915. There is a second unknown wreck in the vicinity which has never been dived and this may be a candidate too. It is a mystery as to why oil and petrol came to the surface but it is possible that the submarine could have discharged materials through a torpedo tube to give *HM Yacht Helga* the impression that she had been hit by a depth charge as a decoy to give the submarine time to escape.

There is a strong possibility that the Admiralty knew that *HM Yacht Helga* had not destroyed a submarine but it would have been entirely detrimental to the morale of the anti-submarine boat crews to have entirely dismissed the claim for a kill. However, the actions and bravery of her crew cannot be taken away and they fully deserved the recognition of the awards made to seven of them by the Admiralty.

**Paper Sources**
Mercantile Navy List 1915
The National Archives of the UK (TNA): Public Record Office (PRO) ADM 137/1516

**Location**
54 02.000 N
04 50.000 W

Between the Calf of Man
and the Chicken Rock

**Vessel**
Steel schooner
London
ON 136,843
138 tons gross, 116 tons net
1900 by Conrad Lühring,
Hammelwarden, Germany
British Admiralty (Fisher,
Alimonda and Company,
manager)
90.9 ft x 21.4 ft x 9.0 ft
27.7 m x 6.5 m x 2.7 m

20.45 hours
5th May 1918

# Sinking of the schooner *Tommi*

The armed drifters *Ocean Gift* and *Fragrance* took the *Tommi*, under Captain David Owens, master, in tow leaving Peel at 7.00 pm on Sunday 5th May 1918. The *Tommi* had left Belfast on Monday 22nd April with a cargo of 195 tons of scrap iron consigned for Liverpool, but was forced to berth at Peel. The wind was blowing a force 4 from the northeast and the weather was clear. At about 8.45 pm when the vessels were between the Chicken Rock and the Calf of Man, about a quarter of a mile from the shore, a large explosion took place after a shell struck the schooner on the quarter throwing up a column of water and splinters. Immediately afterwards, rapid gunfire was being directed at all three vessels. 5 minutes after the first shell hit the *Tommi* she began to settle down aft, having again been struck by further shells. The two naval vessels slipped their tow and headed in the direction of the attacking German submarine, *U-86*, under Oberleutnant zur See Helmut Patzig. The trawlers opened fire, but at this moment a shell from *U-86* raked the schooner from fore to aft and the *Tommi* foundered in a few minutes. The *Ocean Gift* and *Fragrance* stopped their attack on *U-86* and immediately headed for the sinking *Tommi* in the hope of rescuing the crew. The trawler crews could hear cries for help but were unable to see any survivors and so resumed their attack on the submarine.

However, the patrol boats' guns were being outranged by *U-86* and all their shots fell short. The closest the vessels got to *U-86* was about 1 ½ miles. They called off their pursuit and returned to the location where the *Tommi* had gone down. They only found one man, who was bravely trying to swim to shore and they picked him up about 200 yards from the wreckage. The injured man was landed at Port St Mary before proceeding to Douglas for hospital treatment. The other four crewmen had been killed as they tried to launch the small boat. They were:

EGAN, Vincent, seaman
JONES, Owen, cook
JONES, William, mate
OWENS, David, master

The whole incident was witnessed by Mr Haigh and Mr North who were residing on the Calf of Man at the time.

*"About 9 pm on Sunday 5th instant we were at the lower lighthouse Calf of Man looking over the wall when Mr Haigh remarked what a pretty sight referring to two patrol boats with a schooner in tow about a quarter of the distance between the Calf of Man and Chicken's Rock. I saw the top of a conning tower appear above the water to the right of the stack rock from our position, and about a mile away from where we were standing, and about a mile and a quarter from the three vessels mentioned, immediately her deck came above water she commenced firing, the first shot fell fifty yards astern of the schooner, shots were fired in rapid succession, all falling wide, about the tenth shot struck the schooner about amidships on the port side, the schooner veered around to starboard after being struck and was rapidly sinking going down bows first. We only saw one shot actually strike the schooner but several fell very close and may have struck her. After the schooner sank, the submarine proceeded in a southwesterly direction and was consequently lost sight of in the haze."*

The *Tommi* had been captured by the British from the Germans at the outbreak of the war.

## Wreck Site

The probable wreck of the *Tommi* was located in 2012 and lies in 42 metres of water. The length of the wreck is 25 metres, width 7 metres and height 3 metres. The wreck is upright and intact. It is orientated 135/315 degrees. At the date of publication diving operations on the wreck to make a positive identification had not been completed so the exact position of the wreck cannot be published.

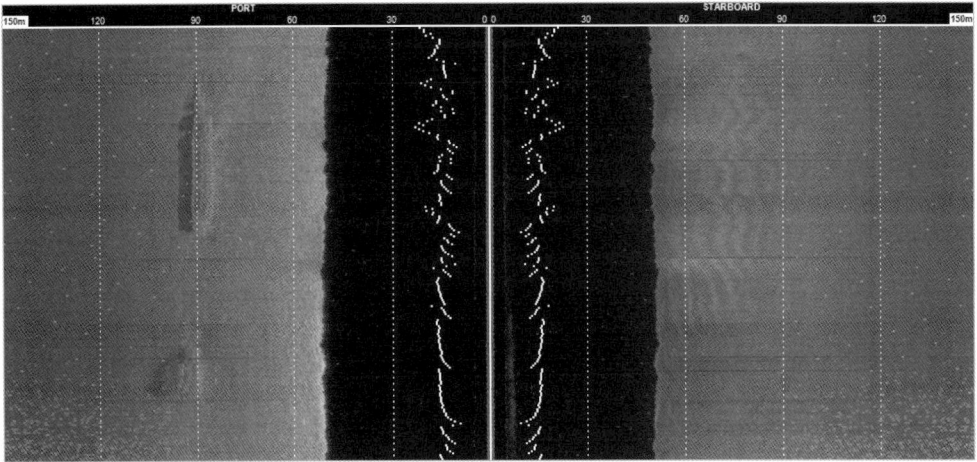

**Above:** Sidescan image of the wreck of the *Tommi* showing a clear shadow indicating the intact nature of the hull. The stern can be seen at the bottom of the image with the bow at the top. The contact below the wreck is the sidescan detecting the wreck head on as the boat was turning before the sonar fish was towed parallel to the wreck to obtain the much clearer upper image.

## Paper Sources

British Vessels Lost at Sea 1914-1918 and 1939-1945, HMSO

Lloyd's Wars Losses, the First World War, Casualties to Shipping through Enemy Causes 1914-1918

The National Archives of the UK (TNA): Public Record Office (PRO) ADM 137/634, ADM 137/1516 ADM 137/2964

World Ship Society

## Paper Sources

Commonwealth War Graves Commission - www.cwgc.org

**Location**
53 57.500 N
04 57.000 W

7 miles southwest
of the Calf of Man

**Vessel**
Steel steamship
Manchester
ON 135,357
1,579 tons gross, 853 tons net
1913 by Murdoch and Murray
Limited, Glasgow
Triple-expansion engine,
211 nhp, Muir and Houston,
Glasgow
Bromsport Steamship Company
Limited (H R Greenhalgh,
manager)
265.5 ft x 38.6 ft x 16.7 ft
80.9 m x 11.8 m x 5.1 m

22.10 hours
15th May 1918

# Steamship *Linmore* rams a German submarine

O n Wednesday 15th May 1918 at 10.10 pm the steamship *Linmore,* under Captain Bilton, master, was in a position 7 miles southwest of the Calf of Man and proceeding in a convoy of three ships escorted by destroyers, steering on a S30W (magnetic) course at about 4 knots. The steamship *Vanaha* was about 6 or 7 cables off the *Linmore's* starboard beam and the steamship *Ikala* beyond her, so that the *Linmore* was the port wing ship.

The night was very dark and Captain Bilton was on the bridge with the first and third officers. Suddenly, Captain Bilton sighted what appeared to be a submarine breaking the surface about 100 feet two points off the *Linmore's* starboard bow, crossing the bows of the steamer. The *Linmore* passed right over the object and a slight shock was felt. Her helm was put hard a port to take her stern over the object but the night was dark so nothing was seen to indicate that the ramming attempt had been successful.

The Shipping Intelligence Officer at Liverpool doubted that the blow was sufficiently heavy to sink the submarine and he surmised that the *Linmore* had only struck the submarine a glancing blow.

**Paper Sources**
Lloyd's Register 1918
The National Archives of the UK (TNA): Public Record Office (PRO) ADM 137/1516

# Attack on a German submarine

On Friday 17th May 1918 at 4.40 am, the armed drifters *Clara Sutton*, *Ocean Gift* and *Fragrance* spotted an object through the haze 2 miles distant. They closed in at full speed and when about 1 mile off, it was seen to be a submarine. At the same time it submerged and at 7.00 am the drifters dropped four depth charges in a wide circle centred around the position where the submarine had dived in position 54 22 N, 04 46 W (about 8 miles north-northwest of Peel). They were ordered to remain in the vicinity for 48 hours and to listen on hydrophones for any movement of the submarine. Further depth charges were dispatched to the drifters but were not needed. The submarine was presumed to have escaped, and was probably the same one that was reported south-southeast of the Chicken Rock, Isle of Man at 6.30 pm the same day.

**Paper Sources**
The National Archives of the UK (TNA): Public Record Office (PRO) ADM137/634

**Location**
54 00.000 N
05 00.000 W

6 miles southwest
of the Calf of Man

**Vessel**
Steel steamship
Whitby
ON 113,733
2,784 tons gross, 1,785 tons net
1902 by J Blumer and Company
Limited, Sunderland
Triple-expansion engine, 263
nhp, J Dickinson and Sons,
Sunderland
Red Cap Steamship Company
Limited (J Good and Sons
Limited, manager)
319.5 ft x 46.0 ft x 21.2 ft
97.4 m x 14.0 m x 6.5 m

08.15 hours
20th May 1918

# Attack on the steamship *Carisbrook*

The steamship *Carisbrook,* under Captain J Hewarth, master, left Gibraltar on Sunday 12th May 1918 bound for Glasgow, as part of a convoy of vessels. The *Carisbrook* parted company with the convoy on Monday 20th May at 4.00 am. At about 8.15 am she was in position 54 00 N, 05 00 W (about 6 miles southwest of the Calf of Man), the weather foggy with a smooth sea, when a German U-Boat was observed. Captain Hewarth at once ran on deck and ordered the course to be altered 8 points to the starboard so that she was heading for land. Within 20 minutes the submarine was lost sight of in the fog and the *Carisbrook* returned to her original course and eventually made her destination of Glasgow.

**Paper Sources**
Lloyd's Register 1916
The National Archives of the UK (TNA): Public Record Office (PRO) ADM137/1516

**Vessel**
Steel "M" class destroyer
1,025 tons displacement
1915 by J S White, Cowes
Steam turbines, 25,000 hp
British Admiralty
273.2 ft x 26.9 ft x 9.1 ft
83.3 m x 8.2 m x 2.8 m

18.56 hours
22nd May 1918

# HMS Moresby attacks a German submarine

A t 6.56 pm on Wednesday 22nd May 1918 *HMS Moresby* was escorting a convoy of merchant vessels in fog in position 54 31 N, 04 18 W (about 6 miles north-northeast of the Point of Ayre). She was about two points off the port front of the convoy when the fog momentarily lifted and her commanding officer together with the officer on watch observed the wake of a submarine and feather from the periscope just at the edge of the fog. Helm was put hard a port and her speed increased to 20 knots. She then dropped a field of depth charges, but nothing further was seen of the submarine which was assumed to have continued to operate.

**Above:** *HMS Moresby* in 1917. (Courtesy of the Imperial War Museum)

**Paper Sources**

The National Archives of the UK (TNA): Public Record Office (PRO) ADM137/1516

# Attack on a German submarine

O n Tuesday 28th May 1918, motor launch *ML201* sighted an object resembling a submarine's periscope 2 miles southeast (magnetic) of Clay Head, Isle of Man, which quickly disappeared. *ML201* and *ML203* closed the position and each vessel dropped one depth charge, 1 cable each side and half a cable ahead of the position where the periscope had disappeared. No results were forthcoming, and after listening for 24 hours on three hydrophones without hearing anything, the two launches continued on their patrol.

**Paper Sources**

The National Archives of the UK (TNA): Public Record Office (PRO) ADM137/634

**Location**
54 07.000 N
05 01.000 W

8 miles northwest
of the Chicken Rock
near the Calf of Man

**Vessel**
Steel steam trawler
Granton (GN14)
ON 123,376
196 tons gross, 77 tons net
1906 by Hall Russell and
Company Limited, Aberdeen
Triple-expansion engine, 70
nhp, Hall Russell and Company
Limited
British Admiralty
115.7 ft x 21.7 ft x 11.6 ft
35.3 m x 6.6 m x 3.5 m

09.00 hours
18th July 1918

# HM Decoy Ship Rosskeen attacks a submarine

The Granton steam trawler *Rosskeen*, was requisitioned in 1914 by the Royal Navy from the owners James and William Lyle of Granton, Edinburgh and converted into a minesweeper. In March 1917, she was converted into a Special Service Ship (or "*Q-ship*" as they were commonly referred to) and rearmed with one 4-inch gun, a 12-pound gun and a 6-pound gun. During the war she used various aliases including *Aldebaran*, *Bendigo II*, *Ethelwulf II*, *General Hunter* and *New Comet*.

HM Decoy Ship *Rosskeen*, under Lieutenant Arthur Rickarde, was lying stationary 8 miles northwest of the Chicken Rock, off the Calf of Man, when at 9.00 am on Thursday 18th July 1918 an enemy submarine was sighted heading south-southwest about 5 miles off the *Rosskeen's* starboard bow. Both trawl boards were quickly recovered and she made full steam to the westward to try and close the submarine while at the same time appearing to be making passage in the direction of Lambay Island, north of Dublin. The submarine was proceeding semi-submerged with no one on deck at about 15 knots. The crew of the *Rosskeen* were ordered to "*action stations*".

By 9.15 am the submarine was only 8,000 yards on the *Rosskeen's* port bow apparently turning away. As the *Rosskeen* could not close any more she opened fire with her 4-inch gun aft and her 12-pounder forward. 5 minutes later the submarine had dived but only after the fourth shot from the 4-inch gun had hit the submarine low down on her conning tower. The final round from the 12-pounder appeared to hit the submarine as well, but the crew of the *Rosskeen* were not certain of a definite hit. A large cloud of black smoke remained where the submarine had disappeared.

The *Rosskeen* proceeded at full steam to the location and went past 200 yards, stopped and listened for 2 minutes. At 9.42 am she steamed full speed in a wide circle on starboard helm from the submarine's last position, dropping four depth charges, three at 150 feet and one at 80 feet and stopped to listen in with her hydrophone. An hour elapsed and nothing had been heard of the submarine. By this time the motor launch *ML201* had appeared on the scene and she took over hydrophone watch. The *Rosskeen* steamed towards land in an attempt to make a wireless transmission, it being impossible to do so in the location where she had attacked the submarine.

Later evidence showed that the submarine continued to operate so must have received only slight damage from the shell fired by the *Rosskeen's* 4-inch gun.

**Paper Sources**
The National Archives of the UK (TNA): Public Record Office (PRO) ADM137/1517
Mercantile Navy List 1915

# The Final Offensive

During the spring of 1917 the U-Boats had been destroying one ship for every 2 days spent on patrol. By the early summer of 1918 this had dropped to one ship for every 14 days on patrol and the tide of war was changing in the favour of the Allies. Yet the German High Command still thought that they could win the war and in June 1918 placed an order for the construction of a further 124 U-Boats, none of which would be ready for service before January 1919. Despite the rapidly rising U-Boat losses Admiral Reinhard Scheer still maintained that *"we must and we will succeed."*

After the lull in U-Boat activity around the Isle of Man during the summer months of 1918, the autumn saw the final brief swansong of the U-Boat offensive in the Irish Sea. The largest ship sunk off the Isle of Man during the war, the steamship *Barrister,* was claimed by *UB-64* on 19th September.

Tragically, on 10th October *RMS Leinster* was sunk off Dublin by *UB-123* with appalling loss of life. A number of bodies, from the more than 500 crew, gun crews and passengers who lost their lives, were later washed ashore on the coast of the Isle of Man. The sinking of the *Leinster* had potentially jeopardised the peace talks between Germany and the Allies. On 14th October, US President Woodrow Wilson told the German government that, *"There can be no peace as long as Germany attacks passenger ships."*

However, the land war on the Western Front moved swiftly during October 1918 as the British army smashed through the Hindenburg Line, with massive German casualties. The German military position had collapsed.

Sick of the Kaiser and his militarists, German politicians convinced a reluctant Admiral Scheer to abandon the U-Boat campaign and on 21st October a signal was sent to all U-Boats at sea ordering them to cease all attacks on passenger ships. Sadly, the message came too late to save the passenger/cargo steamer *Dundalk* which had been torpedoed and sunk off the south of the Isle of Man a week earlier with heavy loss of life.

The war came to an end on Armistice Day on 11th November but the U-Boat offensive was still to claim one more victim off the Isle of Man with the sinking of the steamship *Calista* in January 1919 possibly by a German mine dislodged by winter storms.

## Location
54 05.860 N
05 07.266 W

9 miles west ½ north
of the Calf of Man

## Vessel
Steel steamship
Liverpool
ON 137,498
4,952 tons gross
1916 by Russell and Company,
Port Glasgow
Triple-expansion engine, 474
nhp, J G Kincaird and Company
Limited, Greenock
Charente Steamship Company
Limited (T and J Harrison,
manager)
404.8 ft x 52.2 ft x 27.4 ft
123.4 m x 15.9 m x 8.4 m
Ex Saint Hugo

03.10 hours
19th September 1918

# Sinking of the steamship *Barrister*

The *Barrister,* under Captain Lawrence Joseph French, master, crossed the Liverpool Bar at 8.00 pm on Wednesday 18th September 1918 bound from Liverpool for Glasgow and then the West Indies, with a general cargo and mails weighing 1,200 tons. She immediately started steaming on a zigzag pattern as she made her way across the Irish Sea. Her route instructions were to pass 10 miles south of the Chicken Rock, then 9 ½ miles to the northwest of Crammag Head, near the Mull of Galloway and then 3 ½ miles to the east of Ailsa Craig in the outer Clyde.

It was a fine, clear night with a full moon and a freshening wind from the west-southwest. The *Barrister* was in a position 9 miles west ½ north from the Chicken Rock, when about 3.00 am on Thursday 19th September Captain French went down from the bridge to the chart room. He was laying down bearings on the chart ready for the next leg of the zigzag pattern when at 3.10 am he heard the sound of a torpedo exploding on the port side of his ship abreast of the mainmast. He immediately ran back to the bridge. The second officer had been in charge of the bridge when the torpedo struck and even before Captain French had made the bridge, the second officer had already stopped the engine.

Captain French said to the second officer, *"Don't abandon the ship yet till we see what condition she is in".* Noticing that the ship was heeling over heavily to port and settling down rapidly aft Captain French gave the order to abandon ship and rang off the engine on the telegraph. The second officer ran to the starboard boat ready to launch it, while Captain French instructed the wireless operator to send an SOS and the ship's position. No message was broadcast, however, as it was discovered that the aerial had been carried away in the explosion. Captain French then ran to his cabin in order to destroy all confidential documents which were in the safe. However, before he could destroy them, he could see that the *Barrister* was about to sink and instead he saved his life by jumping over board. The *Barrister* then righted herself before sinking stern first. Captain French succeeded in getting hold of a piece of floating wreckage and then after a few minutes managed to clamber aboard the water-logged port lifeboat which was floating close by and had been launched by three firemen. It transpired that the second officer had been unsuccessful in his attempt to launch the starboard boat as it had been damaged by the davits. The port lifeboat then continued to pick up survivors from the sea.

A quarter of an hour later the German submarine *UB-64*, under Oberleutnant zur See Ernst Krieger, surfaced. She came up alongside the boat containing Captain French and Oberleutnant zur See Krieger asked Captain French for the name of his ship, where bound, where from and tonnage. Captain French gave him only the *Barrister's* net tonnage and no other information. However, some of the other men in the boat gave Oberleutnant zur See Krieger the answers that he wanted. Captain French asked for assistance but was ignored and the *UB-64* shortly afterwards submerged and headed in a westerly direction.

The lifeboat then came across Signalman W E Rippin who first asked if there was room for him in the boat. It was only when Captain French replied *"Yes"* that the signalman climbed in to the boat. He was not wearing a lifebelt. An hour later, Captain French asked all hands to leave the boat so that it could be baled out as they had been standing in the boat with the water up to their waists. Signalman Rippin was the first into the water, but most of the other men refused, with only Captain French, the second officer, third officer and second engineer joining Signalman Rippin in the water. Therefore it was impossible for the boat to be baled out properly and so they all climbed back in again. Signalman Rippin's meritorious conduct continued as he held the dying cabin boy, Reginald Greenfield, in his arms and clear of the water for nearly half an hour before the cabin boy finally died. Two other men also died in the lifeboat.

At 7.15 am the steamship *Ardri*, of Dublin, under Captain Maclean, master, arrived on the scene and was able to take the seventeen survivors and three bodies in the lifeboat on board. The *Ardri* also picked up the two gunners, James Cuthbertson, RNVR and Harold Wood, RNVR, who were on the floating gun platform and a fireman who was clinging to a hatch. All twenty survivors and the three bodies were then taken to Douglas on the Isle of Man by the *Ardri*. Out of the *Barrister's* crew of 45 men, two gunners, two signal men and a pilot, 26 men lost their lives either through the explosion of the torpedo or by drowning as the ship sank and three men in the lifeboat through hypothermia.

The body of second steward Frederick Buckley, aged 38 years, was later recovered from the sea off the Isle of Man and buried at Kirk Christ Rushen. A further three unidentified bodies were found at the Sloc north of Port Erin, at Andreas and at Santon.

The men who died on the *Barrister* were:

ALI, Aman, sailor

BROWN, Thomas, donkeyman

BRYCE, D, telegraphist

BUCKLEY, Frederick, second steward

CAMP, Peter, boatswain

CHEETHAM, William, wireless operator

COOK, John George, first engineer

COSSU, A, boatswain

DEVOY, Alexander, able seaman

GILBERT, P, sailor

GREENFIELD, Reginald Victor, cabin boy

HAFFEY, William John, sailor

HALSALL, Thomas Edward, third engineer

HAZELDENE, W, fireman

HENDERSON, John, able seaman

JONES, Thomas, fireman

KING, Charles Leo, second cook

LARSEN, W, lamps

LEITCH, Campbell Petrie, fireman

McGOLDRICK, Jas Patrick, fireman

MORGAN, Peter Francis, first mate

PARKER, Edward, chief steward

REVILL, William, fireman

ROGERS, William John Brenton, carpenter

THORNLEY, William B, signalman

TROTMAN, Arthur, leading seaman

VEALL, Archibald, purser

VOS, H C, ship's cook

YOUNG, Richard, greaser

## Wreck Site

Latitude 54 05.860 N, Longitude 05 07.266 W

The probable wreck of the *Barrister* lies in 97 metres of water. The length of wreck is 150 metres, width 20 metres and height 18 metres. The wreck lies on a muddy seabed.

## Paper Sources

British Merchant Vessels sunk by U-Boats in the 1914-1918 War, Tennent

British Vessels Lost at Sea 1914-1918 and 1939-1945, HMSO

Dictionary of Disasters at Sea during the Age of Steam, Hocking

Isle of Man Examiner Saturday 28.09.1918. Manx National Heritage

Lloyd's Register 1914

Lloyd's Wars Losses, the First World War, Casualties to Shipping through Enemy Causes 1914-1918

Rushen Parish Burial Register 1712–1968, Manx National Heritage

Sea Breezes p.312 1977

The National Archives of the UK (TNA): Public Record Office (PRO) ADM 137/2964 and ADM137/1517

## Internet Sources

Commonwealth War Graves Commission - www.cwgc.org

Great War Forum - 1914-1918.invisionzone.com

**Location**
53 47.210 N
04 40.610 W

46 miles northwest by west
½ west of the Liverpool Bar
Lightship; 15 miles south
of the Calf of Man

**Vessel**
Steel steamship
Dundalk
ON 107,003
794 tons gross, 327 tons net
1899 by A and J Inglis, Glasgow
Triple-expansion engine, 283
nhp, A and J Inglis, Glasgow
Dundalk and Newry Steam
Packet Company (S J Cocks,
manager)
236.0 ft x 32.1 ft x 15.2 ft
72.0 m x 9.8 m x 4.6 m

11.20 hours
14th October 1918

# Sinking of the steamship *Dundalk*

O n Thursday 6th December 1917, the *Dundalk,* when bound from Liverpool for Dundalk, was attacked by a German submarine, but survived.

However, at 11.20 pm on Monday 14th October 1918, whilst on a voyage from Liverpool to Dundalk, with 150 tons of general cargo, the *Dundalk,* under Captain Hugh O'Neill, master, was torpedoed in the port side of her engine room by the German submarine *U-90*, under Kapitänleutnant Heinrich Jeß, to the south of the Isle of Man. She had been zigzagging since leaving Liverpool Bar, but there was bright moonlight, clear visibility and calm seas at the time enabling the submarine to see its target easily. The explosion was described by survivors to have practically blown her to pieces. The *Dundalk* sank immediately in only 4 minutes. The ship's company numbered 32 persons, consisting of 24 crewmen, three gunners, four cattlemen and one passenger, the general manager of the company, Mr Samuel J Cocks. The two main lifeboats were destroyed by the explosion, but there were two life rafts on deck, which floated off as the vessel foundered. However, most of the crew were left struggling in the water.

A collier steamer then appeared on the scene. Survivors from the *Dundalk* tried to hail the steamer, but she continued on her course without rescuing any of the men. The *U-90* was seen close by and, without offering any assistance, headed south and went out of sight. One of the two small rafts contained five men who had to continually bale it out to keep it afloat. Though fortunate to still be alive, the men were starved with hunger, suffered greatly from exposure and were exhausted when picked up some 16 hours later by the Isle of Man Steam Packet Company steamship *Douglas*. The names of the five men were: Francis Deery, James Tuite, Patrick Kearney, John Higgins, first mate, and Patrick Byrne.

Another seven men in the other raft were rescued by the armed steam trawler *Stormcock* at 4.30 pm and landed at Holyhead after having been observed by an aeroplane. These men were Patrick McCourt, Thomas Fitzgerald, Hugh O'Neill, John Mulqueen, P Noonan, Angus Ferguson, gunner, RNR 1987D and Timothy O'Connor, gunner, RNR 8223.

The seventeen crewmen, one passenger, one cattleman and one gunner who perished were:

BENNETT, Edward, fireman
COCKS, Samuel J, company general manager
CREEGAN, Margaret, stewardess
FOX, Joseph, cattleman
GREY, Harold, gunner, RNVR, Wales, Z/4700
HALFPENNY, Joseph, fireman
HERNON, James, fireman
HUGHES, Patrick, trimmer
JOHNSTON, Edward, chief engineer
KIERAN, John Francis, able seaman
McKEOWN, William, able seaman
MATHEWS, Peter, steward
MELIA, Patrick, second mate
MORGAN, Vincent, greaser
MUCKEAN, John Michael, fireman
O'NEILL, Hugh, master
SLOANE, Peter Valentine, ordinary seaman
STACK, John, fireman
STOWELL, Daniel, quartermaster
TUITE, Thomas, donkeyman

There was some confusion over her position of loss at the time of the *Dundalk's* loss. Official records list her position of loss as 5 miles north-northwest of the Skerries, Anglesey and this was the position given by the survivors landed at Holyhead. However, the survivors who landed at Douglas estimated her position to be 15 miles south of the Chicken Rock. Confirmation of the wreck's identity has proved the latter party to be correct. Indeed in his statement, one of the gun crew who survived, Angus Ferguson, gave the position of loss as 46 miles NW x W ½ W from the Liverpool Bar Light Vessel, a position which tallies with the actual and not the official position of loss from the time.

**Above:** Captain Hugh O'Neil.

**Above:** *SS Dundalk.*

## Wreck Site

Latitude 53 47.210 N, Longitude 04 40.610 W

The confirmed wreck of the *Dundalk* lies in 56 metres of water (artefacts confirming her identity have been recovered by divers). The length of wreck is 80 metres, width 10 metres and height 6 metres. The wreck is split into two pieces, the main section is orientated on an axis of 068/248 degrees with the smaller second piece orientated on an axis of 135/315 degrees. The break exposes the vessel's two boilers and engine room.

## Paper Sources

British Merchant Ships Sunk by U-Boats in the 1914-1918 War, Tennent
British Shipping Fleets, Joseph Fisher and Sons, Fenton and Patterson
British Vessels Lost at Sea 1914-1918 and 1939-1945, HMSO
Dictionary of Disasters at Sea during the Age of Steam, Hocking
Lloyd's Register 1916
Lloyd's Wars Losses, the First World War, Casualties to Shipping through Enemy Causes 1914-1918
Ramsey Courier Friday 25.10.1918. Manx National Heritage
The National Archives of the UK (TNA): Public Record Office (PRO) ADM137/1517, ADM137/634 and ADM137/2964

## Internet Sources

Commonwealth War Graves Commission - www.cwgc.org

**Location**
54 26.500 N
04 50.000 W

11 miles northwest
of Jurby Head

**Vessel**
Steel steamship
Fleetwood
ON 114,299
1,564 tons gross, 659 tons net
1902 by J Brown and Company,
Glasgow
Triple-expansion engine, 340
nhp, J Brown and Company,
Glasgow
Lancashire and Yorkshire and
London and Northwest Railway
Company
315.0 ft x 38.2 ft x 16.7 ft
96.0 m x 11.6 m x 5.1 m

08.13 hours
22nd October 1918

# Aborted attack on the steamship
## *Duke of Connaught*

The *Duke of Connaught* left Fleetwood on Tuesday 22nd October 1918 bound for Belfast when at 8.13 am the same day in position 54 26.50 N, 04 50.00 W a German submarine was observed about a mile off the port quarter. The master gave orders to put the helm hard a port and brought the submarine right astern. He gave orders to the gunners to open fire with the 13-pound gun. Six rounds were fired, but none of the shots were observed to hit the target. A smoke box was thrown overboard and shortly afterwards the submarine disappeared. The *Duke of Connaught* resumed her original course, but adopted a more acute zigzag pattern.

At 8.40 am when she was in position 54 30 N, 04 52 W the submarine was again sighted crossing from starboard to port quarter, distant about 1¼ miles. The submarine was again brought astern and fire opened on her at a range of 2,000 yards. Only one round was fired, but it did not hit. The submarine submerged and then reappeared later on the steamer's starboard quarter with her conning tower awash. Two further rounds were fired by the *Duke of Connaught* at the submarine and both landed very close to her forcing her to submerge again. Nothing further was seen of the submarine and the *Duke of Connaught* continued on her passage to Belfast.

**Above:** *SS Duke of Connaught.*

## Paper Sources

Lloyd's Register 1916

The National Archives of the UK (TNA): Public Record Office (PRO) ADM137/1517

**Location**
54 32.000 N
04 37.000 W

10 miles northwest by west
from the Point of Ayre

**Vessel**
Steel steamship
Belfast
ON 114,299
468 tons gross, 183 tons net
1909 by Scott and Company,
Bowling
Compound engine, 98 rhp, Ross
and Duncan, Glasgow
Alexander King Limited
160.0 ft x 25.6 ft x 11.3 ft
48.8 m x 7.8 m x 3.4 m

23.45 hours
24th October 1918

# Aborted attack on the steamship *Corbet*

The *Corbet*, under Captain James Bell, master, left Belfast at 6.00 pm on Thursday 24th October 1918 bound for Garston. When in position approximately 10 miles northwest by west from the Point of Ayre at about 11.45 pm, Captain Bell sighted a German submarine right ahead crossing his vessel's bows to port at a distance of about 60 yards.

Captain Bell sent a message to the gun crew aft with the order to stand by and at the same time shouted from the bridge for them to open fire as soon as the sights came on. The *Corbet* then altered course in an attempt to ram the submarine which prevented the gun crew from fixing their sights on the submarine as the gun platform was at the aft end of the *Corbet*. The attempt at ramming the submarine was unsuccessful so Captain Bell altered course to starboard which brought the submarine in view of the gun crew, who opened fire immediately. Four rounds were fired. The first shot was observed to fall about 2 feet to the right of the submarine. The second round, being pointed common ammunition, was fired and a slight explosion was heard and a dull blue flare was seen. The third and fourth rounds, which were high explosive ammunition, were fired with unknown results.

The submarine was roughly 30 to 40 yards away when fire was first opened by the *Corbet*. However, the submarine was moving at high speed and firing rockets into the air. By the third shot the submarine had disappeared from sight. On the *Corbet* going to starboard, a red light was observed on the after part of the conning tower and the gun was laid accordingly, but before the gun could be fired, the light disappeared.

**Paper Sources**

Lloyd's Register 1916
The National Archives of the UK (TNA): Public Record Office (PRO) ADM137/1517

**Location**
53 18.867 N
05 47.571 W

8 miles east-southeast
of the Kish Light Vessel,
off Dublin

**Vessel**
Steel steamship
Dublin
ON 104,974
2,646 tons gross, 1,101 tons net
1897 by Laird Brothers,
Birkenhead
Triple-expansion engine, 529 nhp,
Laird Brothers, Birkenhead
City of Dublin Steam Packet
Company Limited, Dublin
360.0 ft x 41.5 ft x 27.3 ft
109.8 m x 12.7 m x 8.3 m

00.00 hours
3rd - 17th November 1918

# Bodies recovered from the sinking of RMS Leinster

RMS *Leinster,* under Captain William Birch, master, departed from Kingstown (now Dun Laoghaire) on Thursday 10th October 1918 at 8.53 am bound for Holyhead with 771 crew, postal workers and passengers on board. Over 400 of the passengers were military personnel either going on or returning from leave.

At 9.50 am, when she was about 8 miles east-southeast of the Kish Light Vessel off Dublin, Captain Birch had just given the order to commence zigzagging when the track of a torpedo was seen coming abaft the beam on her port side. The helm was put hard a port and the starboard engine rung full speed astern. The torpedo struck well forward and was followed 6 minutes later by a second torpedo which struck amidships on her starboard side. Both torpedoes were fired by *UB-123*, under Oberleutnant zur See Robert Ramm. The *Leinster* began to settle down rapidly on her port side and went down by the bow with her starboard propeller in the air before finally disappearing beneath the waves. 501 people lost their lives in this terrible tragedy so close to the end of the war. *UB-123* was lost 9 days later in the North Sea on her way back to Germany after she hit a British mine. All 36 hands went down with her.

The body of Lance Corporal Harold Wilkinson, Royal Welsh Fusiliers (service number 71,605), came ashore on the coast of the Isle of Man on Sunday 3rd November. His family resided at 10 Trevelyan Street, Eccles, Manchester.

Coast watchers J T Kinrade and Richard Taylor, picked up the body of Private Horace

Cook, East Kent Regiment, 10th Battalion (service number 58,356) in Port St Mary Bay on Thursday 7th November. He had been returning from leave at Ballina in Ireland to his way home at 4 Murray Road, Wimbledon, London. His remains were interred at Douglas Borough Cemetery. Two more bodies were found on the west coast of the Isle of Man. The first was that of Second Lieutenant Victor Frederick Sloper, Wiltshire Regiment, 4th Battalion. The second was that of Private George Lutton, Royal Munster Fusiliers, 6th Battalion (service number 5,251). His remains were interred at Kirk Patrick.

About 7.00 am on the morning of Friday 8th November, the body of a soldier was washed ashore in Castletown Bay, just under the Big Cellar. Papers showed the man to be Private William Herbert Hutchinson, Border Regiment (service number 57,451). He was the son of Mr H W and Mrs R Hutchinson of 31 Willersley Street, Nottingham. His remains were interred at Douglas Borough Cemetery. The same morning the body of a man was washed ashore in Douglas Bay, just opposite the slipway at the foot of Summer Hill. The body had a shamrock tattooed on the right wrist, but no identification could be made. The same day a third body, that of a sailor, was washed ashore at Strand Hall, Arbory. Again no identification could be made.

On Saturday 9th November the body of Private Michael Daniel Biggane, Canadian Army Service Corps (service number 2,738), was found at Ballelby, near Peel. His mother, who resided at Waterford, was communicated with, and the remains were removed there for interment at Ballylaneen (St Anne) Catholic churchyard. On the same day, the body of Private E H Dunn, Royal Defence Corps, whose home was at 31 Merchant Road, Dublin, was brought ashore at Port Erin. He was returning to his regiment from leave. The unidentified body of a woman of between 20 and 30 years of age was also found at Fenella Beach, Peel on Saturday 9th November.

The next day Sunday 10th November on the beach between Peel and Glen Maye, Robert Hampton found the body of Corporal Michael Carroll, Royal Army Medical Corps (service number 53,051) and his remains were later interred at Kirk Patrick near Peel. He was the son of Thomas and Bridget Carroll, of 10 Kilmacud Road, Stillorgan, Dublin. Later the same day the unidentified body of a woman was picked up at Niarbyl on the west coast of the Isle of Man.

A body was picked up at Little Carrick, Port St Mary harbour on Saturday 16th November. It was that of Private Richard Jones, Royal Welsh Fusiliers (service number 74,314). His body was later interred at Llanllyfni (Gorphwysfa) Cemetery, Gwynedd, North Wales.

On Sunday 17th November the body of Private Thomas Cardiff, Royal Air Force (service number 296,972) was washed ashore at Cass-ny-Hawin, in the parish of Santon on the southeast coast of the Isle of Man. He was the son of John Cardiff, 14 Behan's Cottages, James' Street, Dublin. His body was interred at Douglas Borough Cemetery.

## Wreck Site

Latitude 53 18.867 N, Longitude 05 47.571 W

The confirmed wreck of the *Leinster* lies in 28 metres of water (artefacts confirming her identity have been recovered by divers). The length of wreck is 75 metres, width 16 metres and height 4 metres. The stern section has broken away or is buried in a sand wave. About 54 metres of the wreck remains relatively intact although the superstructure has collapsed. The wreck is orientated on an axis of 005/185 degrees with the bow to the north.

## Paper Sources

British Merchant Ships Sunk by U-Boats in the 1914-1918 War, Tennent
British Vessels Lost at Sea 1914-1918 and 1939-1945, HMSO
Dictionary of Disasters at Sea during the Age of Steam, Hocking
Isle of Man Times Saturday 09.11.1918, 16.1.1918. and 23.11.1918. Manx National Heritage
Lloyd's Register 1916
Lloyd's Wars Losses, the First World War, Casualties to Shipping through Enemy Causes 1914-1918
The National Archives of the UK (TNA): Public Record Office (PRO) ADM137/1517

## Internet Sources

Commonwealth War Graves Commission - www.cwgc.org

Off the Calf of Man

**Vessel**
Steel steamship
Glasgow
ON 115,671
229 tons gross, 121 tons net
1902 by C Connell and Company,
Whitinch
Compound engine, McKie and
Baxter, Glasgow
Preston Steam Navigation
Company Limited (Becker and
Company Limited, manager)
124.0 ft x 22.0 ft x 11.0 ft
37.8 m x 6.7 m x 3.4 m

00.00 hours
10th January 1919

# Probable mining of the steamship *Calista*

The *Calista* was originally a steam yacht before being converted to a coasting steamer presumably in response to the lack of shipping and high freight charges precipitated by the First World War.

The *Calista*, under Captain Alfred Corkill (originally of Port St Mary), master, left Preston on Monday 6th January 1919 bound for Dublin, presumably with a cargo of coal. The bad weather in the channel forced her to take shelter in the north end of Ramsey Bay off Cranstal where she was seen by coastguards on Tuesday 7th January.

On Friday 10th January, she recommenced her journey to Dublin and was never seen again. Later the same day, a small boat belonging to her was washed ashore on Langness. It was presumed all of her crew of nine men had been lost.

The *Calista* is officially listed as a war loss despite the fact that she sank after the war in 1919. The most probable explanation for her loss is that she hit a mine and sank off either Langness or the Calf of Man. After the news of her loss, minesweepers made a search for mines off Langness. Her route took her over areas where mines had been laid and successfully used by the Germans and it is possible that the winter storm she had sheltered from could have dislodged mines previously missed by minesweepers.

The men who died on the *Calista* were:

ASHCROFT, Albert, fireman
CORKILL, Alfred Harrison, master
DAGGER, Walter, second engineer
FEARN, Maitland, first engineer
LEMMON, Alexander, steward
MITCHELL, Samuel, boatswain
MURPHY, William, fireman
PARRY, William, mate
YOUNG, Alfred, able seaman

## Wreck Site
Latitude 54 01.752 N, Longitude 05 00.790 W

The possible wreck of the *Calista* lies in 67 metres of water. The length of wreck is 35 metres, width 6 metres and height 4 metres. The wreck is a small steamer carrying a cargo of coal in a single hold. The stern section is fairly intact but forward sections are almost flat to the seabed. Large amounts of old trawl netting are caught on a steel structure near to the boiler that rises a further 4 metres above the top of the wreck. The boiler and a compound steam engine are positioned at the stern of the vessel. There is no sign of the propeller. It is concluded that this wreck may well be that of the *Calista* owing to its size, configuration, cargo and location. The *Calista* could not have been lost off Langness as no unidentified wreck matching her description is known to lie off Langness.

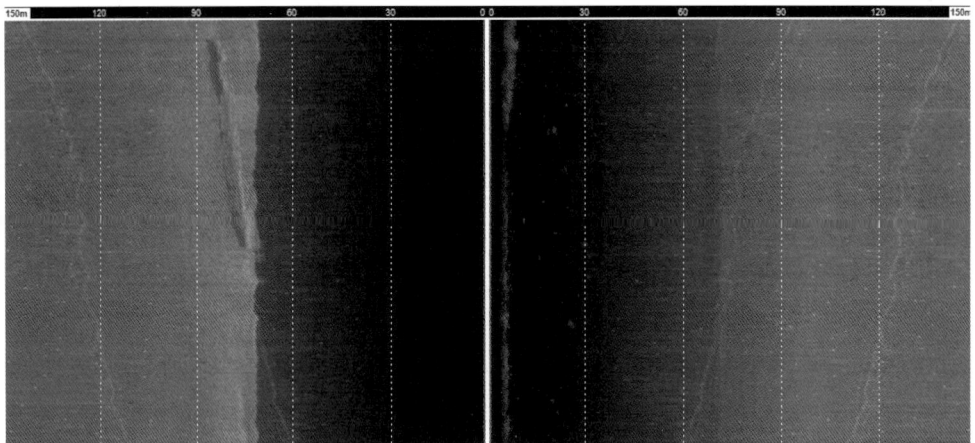

**Above:** Sidescan image of the possible wreck of the *SS Calista* off the Calf of Man.

## Paper Sources
Isle of Man Weekly Times Saturday 25.01.1919 Manx National Heritage
Mercantile Navy List 1910
Ramsey Courier Friday 24.01.1919. and 21.02.1919. Manx National Heritage
World Ship Society

## Internet Sources
Commonwealth War Graves Commission - www.cwgc.org

# List of events

## 1915

| | |
|---|---|
| 30 January | Sinking of the steamship *Kilcoan* |
| 20 February | Sinking of the steamship *Downshire* |
| 9 March | Sinking of the steamship *Princess Victoria* |
| 19 March | *HMS Bayano* – recovery of bodies and inquests |
| 28 August | Destruction of *RN Yacht Dolores* |

## 1916

| | |
|---|---|
| 4 November | Sinking of the steamship *Skerries* |
| 18 December | Disappearance of the steamship *Opal* |
| 19 December | Sinking of the steamship *Liverpool* |
| 21 December | Minefield off the Calf of Man |

## 1917

| | |
|---|---|
| 15 February | Mining of the steamship *Celtic* |
| 10 March | Disappearance of the steamship *G A Savage* |
| 10 May | Foundering of the steam tug *PT1* |
| 24 July | Sinking of the steamship *Mikelis* |
| 25 July | Attack on *HMS Berwick* |
| 9 October | Sinking of *HMS Champagne* |
| 10 October | Disappearance of *HMT Waltham* |
| 3 November | Attack on the steamship *Atlantian* |
| 6 December | Attack on the steamship *Dundalk* |
| 13 December | Sinking of *HMS Stephen Furness* |

## 1918

| | |
|---|---|
| 2 January | Sinking of the steamship *Nadejda* |
| 7 February | Sinking of the steamship *Limesfield* |
| 7 February | Sinking of the steamship *Ben Rein* |
| 7 February | Sinking of the steamship *Ardbeg* |
| 11 February | Sinking of *HMS Cullist* |

| | |
|---|---|
| 20 February | *USS Downes* attacks a German submarine |
| 23 February | Attack on the fishing vessel *Girl Emily* |
| 24 February | Sinking of the steamship *Sarpfos* |
| 26 February | Sinking of the steamship *Dalewood* |
| 27 February | Sinking of the steamship *Largo* |
| 2 March | Sinking of the steamship *Carmelite* |
| 2 March | Sinking of the motor ketch *Bessy* |
| 2 March | Sinking of the steamship *Kenmare* |
| 3 March | Sinking of the steamship *Romeo* |
| 9 March | Sinking of the fishing smack *Marguerite* |
| 10 March | *HMS Michael* attacks a German submarine |
| 10 March | Sinking of the fishing ketch *Wave* |
| 10 March | Sinking of the fishing smack *Sunrise* |
| 22-30 March | Bodies recovered from the steamship *Sea Gull* |
| 26 March | Attack on the steamship *Cliffmore* |
| 28 March | Attack on the steamship *Leafield* |
| 28 March | Sinking of the steamship *Inkosi* |
| 29 March | Attack on the steamship *Oranian* |
| 31 March | Sinking of the steamship *Conargo* |
| 31 March | Attack on the steamship *Milwaukee* |
| 31 March | Attack on the steamship *Celtic* |
| 2 April | *HMD Dick Whittington* attacks a submarine |
| 3 April | *HMS PC61* attacks a German submarine |
| 4 April | Possible submarine kill by *HM Yacht Helga* |
| 5 May | Sinking of the schooner *Tommi* |
| 15 May | Steamship *Linmore* rams a German submarine |
| 17 May | Attack on a German submarine |
| 20 May | Attack on the steamship *Carisbrook* |
| 22 May | *HMS Moresby* attacks a German submarine |
| 28 May | Attack on a German submarine |
| 18 July | *HM Decoy Ship Rosskeen* attacks a submarine |
| 19 September | Sinking of the steamship *Barrister* |
| 14 October | Sinking of the steamship *Dundalk* |
| 22 October | Aborted attack on the steamship *Duke of Connaught* |
| 24 October | Aborted attack on the steamship *Corbet* |
| 3-17 November | Bodies recovered from the sinking of *RMS Leinster* |

## 1919

| | |
|---|---|
| 10 January | Probable mining of the steamship *Calista* |

# Index of lives lost

| NAME | VESSEL | NAME | VESSEL |
|------|--------|------|--------|
| AHERN, Michael | *Kenmare* | BOYER, George | *HMS Champagne* |
| AHMAD | *Dalewood* | BRADSHAW, Edward | *HMS Champagne* |
| ALCOCK, William | *HMS Champagne* | BRADY, Joseph | *HMS Champagne* |
| ALDWINCKLE, Harry | *Conargo* | BROWN, James | *HMS Champagne* |
| ALI, Aman | *Barrister* | BROWN, John | *HMS Stephen Furness* |
| ALLEN, Joseph | *Romeo* | BROWN, John David | *HMS Stephen Furness* |
| ANDERSON, Herbert | *Romeo* | BROWN, John E | *Dalewood* |
| ASHCROFT, Albert | *Calista* | BROWN, Thomas | *Barrister* |
| ASKARI, Said | *Dalewood* | BROWNE, Ernest | *HMS Cullist* |
| ASKEW, John Amos | *Dalewood* | BRYCE, D | *Barrister* |
| ASTON, Albert E | *Kenmare* | BRYDEN, Henry R | *Skerries* |
| ATKIN, Edward | *PT1* | BUCKETT, Richard Henry | *HMS Stephen Furness* |
| ATKINSON, John Ernest | *HMS Stephen Furness* | BUCKLEY, Frederick | *Barrister* |
| BACH, Thomas | *HMS Stephen Furness* | BUCKROYD, John Edwin | *HMS Stephen Furness* |
| BAILEY, Frederick Maurice | *HMS Champagne* | BUNTING, John | *HMS Stephen Furness* |
| BARGEWELL, George | *Romeo* | BURKE, Joseph | *HMS Stephen Furness* |
| BARKER, Arthur | *HMS Stephen Furness* | BURNS, Thomas | *HMS Stephen Furness* |
| BARLOW, Thomas Walter | *HMS Stephen Furness* | CAMP, George Robert | *HMS Stephen Furness* |
| BARTELL, John | *HMS Cullist* | CAMP, Peter | *Barrister* |
| BATES, Leonard | *HMS Cullist* | CAMPBELL, Abraham Stewart | *Opal* |
| BELL, Andrew | *HMS Stephen Furness* | CAMPBELL, Duncan | *HMT Waltham* |
| BENNETT, Edward | *Dundalk* | CAMPBELL, Roderick | *Opal* |
| BIGGANE, Michael Daniel | *Leinster* | CARDIFF, Thomas | *Leinster* |
| BIRD, George | *HMS Champagne* | CARNEY, Arthur | *Romeo* |
| BIRKINSHAW, Ronald | *Romeo* | CARR, Horatius Hartley | *HMS Cullist* |
| BLACKLOCK, Peter | *Kenmare* | CARR, John | *Romeo* |
| BLAIR, George | *Romeo* | CARROLL, Michael | *Leinster* |
| BLORE, George William | *HMS Stephen Furness* | CATTERMOLE, Christopher Stanley | *HMS Stephen Furness* |
| BOBBINS, William | *HMS Stephen Furness* | CHATERIS | *PT1* |
| BODIE, Robert | *Celtic* | CHEETHAM, William | *Barrister* |
| BOND, Charles | *HMS Stephen Furness* | CHURCHHOUSE, Arthur F | *HMS Stephen Furness* |
| BONWICK, George James | *Dalewood* | CLAYTON, Fred | *HMS Stephen Furness* |
| BOWEN, Stephen | *Kenmare* | | |

| NAME | VESSEL | NAME | VESSEL |
|------|--------|------|--------|
| CLAYTON, Joseph | *HMS Champagne* | EVANS, William | *HMS Stephen Furness* |
| CLEARY, Philip | *G A Savage* | FAIRMANIER, Edwin A | *Dalewood* |
| COCKBURN, John | *HMS Cullist* | FEARN, Maitland | *Calista* |
| COCKS, Samuel J | *Dundalk* | FENNESSAY, Patrick | *Kenmare* |
| COHEN, Bernard | *HMS Champagne* | FEWSTER, Charles Frederick | *HMT Waltham* |
| COLEMAN, Michael | *Kenmare* | FITZGERALD, James | *Kenmare* |
| COMPTON, Thomas | *HMS Champagne* | FOX, Joseph | *Dundalk* |
| COOK, Horace | *Leinster* | FOXON, Harold Lewis | *HMS Stephen Furness* |
| COOK, John George | *Barrister* | FRACKLETON, William | *Inkosi* |
| COOK, Percy | *HMS Cullist* | FRISWELL, John Roderick Thomas | *HMS Stephen Furness* |
| COOPER, Joseph | *HMS Champagne* | FROMM, Thoedore Howard | *Romeo* |
| CORCORAN, Patrick John | *Kenmare* | GAHAN, Thomas | *HMS Stephen Furness* |
| CORKILL, Alfred Harrison | *Calista* | GALBRAITH, David | *Opal* |
| CORVAN, Patrick Lawrence | *HMS Cullist* | GALVIN, Joseph | *HMS Stephen Furness* |
| COSSU, A | *Barrister* | GARVEY, Daniel | *Liverpool* |
| COSTELLO, J | *Liverpool* | GARWOOD, Sidney George | *HMS Cullist* |
| COX, Valentine | *HMS Stephen Furness* | GAY, Albert Stephen | *HMS Cullist* |
| CRANG, Walter | *HMS Stephen Furness* | GEORGE, Alastair Farquhar | *HMS Stephen Furness* |
| CREEGAN, Margaret | *Dundalk* | GERAGHTY, James Raymond | *HMS Bayano* |
| CROWTHER, Charles | *Romeo* | GILBERT, P | *Barrister* |
| DAGGER, Walter | *Calista* | GILLAN, Michael | *HMS Cullist* |
| DALEY, James | *HMS Stephen Furness* | GILLEN, J P | *Liverpool* |
| DARRAGH, Bernard | *Sea Gull* | GLEAVE, William Edwin | *Celtic* |
| DARRAGH, James | *Sea Gull* | GOOD, John Jeremiah | *Kenmare* |
| DARRAGH, Thomas | *Opal* | GOULD, William Henry Felix | *HMS Stephen Furness* |
| DAVIES, Sidney Lewis | *HMS Stephen Furness* | GRANT, Geoffrey Joseph | *Kenmare* |
| DEADMAN, Robert Methven | *Romeo* | GREEN, John Henry | *PT1* |
| DEAKIN, Albert | *HMS Champagne* | GREENFIELD, Reginald Victor | *Barrister* |
| DEAN, Stanley Edwin | *HMS Cullist* | GREY, Harold | *Dundalk* |
| DEEGAN, James Clark | *Conargo* | GROVES, Walter William | *HMS Stephen Furness* |
| DEELEY, Walter | *HMS Stephen Furness* | GRUNDY, Andrew | *Conargo* |
| DELEA, Michael | *Kenmare* | GULLY, Lewis Vincent | *HMS Cullist* |
| DENT, George | *HMS Champagne* | GUSTAFSON, Hugo | *Romeo* |
| DEVOY, Alexander | *Barrister* | HAFFEY, William John | *Barrister* |
| DOUBLEDAY, George Hambrook Dean | *HMS Cullist* | HALFPENNY, Joseph | *Dundalk* |
| DUNN, E H | *Leinster* | HALL, Frederick | *HMS Cullist* |
| DUNTHORNE, Alfred | *Sea Gull* | HALL, Joseph William | *HMS Stephen Furness* |
| DUPREY, Alfred Frank | *HMS Stephen Furness* | HALSALL, Thomas Edward | *Barrister* |
| DYOTT, Kenelm Mitchill | *HMS Stephen Furness* | HAMMOND, Harry George | *HMS Stephen Furness* |
| EDWARDS, Charles William | *HMS Champagne* | HANNAH, Hugh | *Opal* |
| EGAN, Vincent | *Tommi* | HARDEN, Walter Marshall | *HMS Champagne* |
| ETCHELLS, William | *HMS Stephen Furness* | HARDLEY, George H | *G A Savage* |
| EVANS, Vernon Arthur Martin | *HMS Stephen Furness* | | |

| NAME | VESSEL | NAME | VESSEL |
|------|--------|------|--------|
| HARTNETT, W | *Kenmare* | KEENAN, John | *Kenmare* |
| HARVEY, Joseph | *Romeo* | KELLY, William Joseph | *HMS Stephen Furness* |
| HASSAN, A | *Dalewood* | KEMP, Oscar | *Kenmare* |
| HAWORTH, William | *HMS Stephen Furness* | KERSLEY, Walter | *HMS Cullist* |
| HAZELDENE, W | *Barrister* | KIERAN, John Francis | *Dundalk* |
| HELLEYER, A A | *HMS Bayano* | KING, Arthur Grey | *HMS Bayano* |
| HELM, Richard James | *Romeo* | KING, Charles Leo | *Barrister* |
| HEMINGWAY, Wilfred O | *HMS Champagne* | KING, Stanhope | *HMS Champagne* |
| HENDERSON, John | *Barrister* | KRAMMER, Carl Martin | *G A Savage* |
| HENRY, Reginald | *HMS Champagne* | LAMB, John | *HMS Cullist* |
| HERNON, James | *Dundalk* | LARSEN, W | *Barrister* |
| HERTFORD, John | *Inkosi* | LAWES, H B | *HMS Stephen Furness* |
| HESELTINE, Willie | *HMS Stephen Furness* | LAYDEN, William | *HMS Champagne* |
| HINDLEY, Robert Muir | *HMS Cullist* | LEARY, Jerimiah | *HMS Cullist* |
| HINES, Thomas | *Romeo* | LEE, Martin | *Romeo* |
| HOBAN, Richard Edward | *HMS Cullist* | LEE, William Edward | *Dalewood* |
| HODGKINSON, Francis George | *HMS Stephen Furness* | LEITCH, Campbell Petrie | *Barrister* |
| | | LEMMON, Alexander | *Calista* |
| HODGSON, Alexander | *G A Savage* | LEONARD, Frank | *HMS Champagne* |
| HODGSON, Richard | *Dalewood* | LEWIS, Joseph | *HMS Cullist* |
| HOLLAND, Michael Daniel | *HMT Waltham* | LINACRE, John Edward | *Romeo* |
| HONG, Chung | *Skerries* | LONGLEY, John Blyth | *Romeo* |
| HOPKINS, James | *HMS Stephen Furness* | LOVEDAY, Henry | *HMS Stephen Furness* |
| HOWSE, Thomas John Albert | *HMS Stephen Furness* | LUTTON, George | *Leinster* |
| HUGHES, Patrick | *Dundalk* | LYCETT, William Ernest | *HMS Cullist* |
| HUNTER, William Thomas | *HMS Stephen Furness* | LYONS, William | *Kenmare* |
| HUTCHINSON, William Herbert | *Leinster* | McCALLUM, David Crawford | *HMS Stephen Furness* |
| | | McCARTHY, Dennis | *HMS Cullist* |
| HYSLOP, John William | *HMS Champagne* | McCARTIE, Percival Hammond | *Kenmare* |
| JACKSON, Patrick | *Conargo* | | |
| JEFFERS, Charles | *Celtic* | McCRAE, Neil | *Carmelite* |
| JELFS, Raymond Victor John | *HMS Cullist* | McDONALD, James | *HMS Stephen Furness* |
| JOHNSON, Alfred | *HMS Champagne* | McDONALD, Lawrence | *HMS Stephen Furness* |
| JOHNSTON, Edward | *Dundalk* | McDONALD, Stanley Angus | *Celtic* |
| JOHNSTONE, R | *Kenmare* | McDONNELL, Archibald | *Opal* |
| JOINSON, Joseph Henry | *HMS Cullist* | McFADDEN, Robert | *HMS Cullist* |
| JONES, David | *Dalewood* | McGLASSON, William Smith | *HMS Champagne* |
| JONES, Owen | *Tommi* | McGOLDRICK, Jas Patrick | *Barrister* |
| JONES, Richard | *Leinster* | McGREGOR, Alexander Thomson | *HMS Stephen Furness* |
| JONES, Thomas | *Barrister* | | |
| JONES, William | *Tommi* | McINTOSH, Karl | *HMS Stephen Furness* |
| JORDAN, James | *Conargo* | McIVOR, John | *HMS Cullist* |
| JOURNEAUX, Wilfred Redfers | *HMS Champagne* | McKAY, Charles | *Opal* |
| KEARNEY, James | *Romeo* | McKENZIE, John | *HMS Stephen Furness* |
| KEEFE, John | *Kenmare* | | |

| NAME | VESSEL | NAME | VESSEL |
|---|---|---|---|
| McKENZIE, John McDonald | HMS Stephen Furness | MURRAY, John James | Opal |
| McKEOWN, William | Dundalk | NABI, Abdul | Dalewood |
| McLEOD, Arthur | HMS Champagne | NAJAF, Muhammad | HMS Champagne |
| McLOUGHLIN, David | Romeo | NASBET, Thomas | Dalewood |
| McLOUGHLIN, Robert | Kenmare | NEALE, James | Romeo |
| McNAMARA, E | Kenmare | NUGENT, Jas Alfred | Romeo |
| McPHERSON, John Shaw | Opal | OAKES, Albert | HMS Stephen Furness |
| McROBBIE, William | HMS Cullist | O'BRIEN, Andrew | Romeo |
| MacAULAY, John | Kenmare | O'DRISCOLL, Michael John | Kenmare |
| MacKINNON, Neal Shaw | HMS Cullist | OGLE, Thomas Hugh | Kenmare |
| MacLEOD, Donald | PT1 | O'GORMAN, Thomas Christopher | Romeo |
| MacRAE, Alexander | HMS Stephen Furness | | |
| MAGUIRE, Frank | Opal | O'NEILL, Hugh | Dundalk |
| MAIR, James | HMT Waltham | OWENS, David | Tommi |
| MALONE, Henry James | Conargo | PALMER, George Walter | HMS Stephen Furness |
| MANGAN, John | HMS Champagne | PARKER, Edward | Barrister |
| MANSELL, Herbert | HMS Stephen Furness | PARRY, John | Romeo |
| MARIS, Christopher Reginald | HMS Cullist | PARRY, William | Calista |
| MARSH, Robert Wright | HMT Waltham | PATIENCE, John William | HMS Stephen Furness |
| MARSHALL, William A | HMS Champagne | PATTEN, Tom Franklin | HMS Cullist |
| MARTIN, Alfred | HMS Cullist | PECKHAM, William | HMS Champagne |
| MARTIN, Donald | Opal | PERELLO, Vincent | Sea Gull |
| MATHEWS, Peter | Dundalk | PITTS, Albert | Romeo |
| MAWHINNEY, James | HMS Champagne | POWER, Christopher | Conargo |
| MEEHAN, Henry Leo | HMS Stephen Furness | POWER, Thomas | Conargo |
| MELIA, Patrick | Dundalk | RAINFORD, Thomas Henry | HMS Stephen Furness |
| MEREDITH, Arthur Reginald | HMS Stephen Furness | RATCLIFFE, Robert Francis | HMS Stephen Furness |
| MIDDLETON, John William | Romeo | REDFORD, Ralph | HMS Stephen Furness |
| MITCHELL, Samuel | Calista | REED, Cuthbert Reveley | HMS Stephen Furness |
| MOLLOY, Patrick | Romeo | REVILL, William | Barrister |
| MOORE, William | Kenmare | RHODES, Arthur Leslie | HMS Stephen Furness |
| MORGAN, Peter Francis | Barrister | RICH, Herbert Henry | HMS Cullist |
| MORGAN, Vincent | Dundalk | RICHARDSON, Edmund | HMT Waltham |
| MORRIS, S | Conargo | RICHARDSON, George | Celtic |
| MORRISON, John | HMS Stephen Furness | RIDDLE, William George | Dalewood |
| MUCKEAN, John Michael | Dundalk | RITCHIE, Henry | HMS Stephen Furness |
| MUDIE, John Fitzgerald | HMS Stephen Furness | ROBERTSON, A | G A Savage |
| MUHAMMAD, Ali | Dalewood | ROBILLIARD, Ernest | HMS Cullist |
| MUHAMMAD, Hussain | Dalewood | ROBINSON, John | HMS Stephen Furness |
| MULLANEY, John | HMS Stephen Furness | ROBINSON, John | HMS Stephen Furness |
| MURPHY, J | Conargo | ROGERS, Henry Richard | HMS Stephen Furness |
| MURPHY, Thomas | Kenmare | ROGERS, William John Brenton | Barrister |
| MURPHY, William | Calista | | |

| NAME | VESSEL | NAME | VESSEL |
|---|---|---|---|
| ROMANS, William Franklyn | *HMS Stephen Furness* | TALMEY, W F | *HMS Stephen Furness* |
| ROSSBOROUGH, John | *Opal* | TAMURA, T | *Dalewood* |
| ROUTLEDGE, Samuel | *Celtic* | TAYLOR, Francis Thomas | *HMS Stephen Furness* |
| ROWAN, Hugh | *Inkosi* | TAYLOR, James Henry | *HMS Stephen Furness* |
| RYAN, John | *HMS Champagne* | TELFORD, Thomas Butterwicke | *Dalewood* |
| SAID, S | *Dalewood* | | |
| SALEH, Ali | *Dalewood* | THOMAS, Tom | *G A Savage* |
| SHAW, Alan C | *Kenmare* | THOMAS, William E | *HMS Champagne* |
| SHAW, John | *HMS Champagne* | THOMPSON, Jacob John | *HMS Champagne* |
| SHEATHER, Alfred Reginald | *HMS Cullist* | THORNLEY, William B | *Barrister* |
| SHIRLEY, William | *HMS Stephen Furness* | THORPE, James | *HMS Stephen Furness* |
| SHOEBOTTOM, Samuel Joseph | *HMS Cullist* | TOLAN, William | *HMT Waltham* |
| | | TROTMAN, Arthur | *Barrister* |
| SIMS, Horace W | *HMS Champagne* | TUCKER, Leonard Francis | *HMS Stephen Furness* |
| SKINNER, John | *HMS Stephen Furness* | TUITE, Thomas | *Dundalk* |
| SLOANE, Peter Valentine | *Dundalk* | TURNER, John | *Carmelite* |
| SLOPER, Victor Frederick | *Leinster* | TURNER, Thomas Thompson | *HMS Cullist* |
| SMITH, Alfred Albert | *HMS Stephen Furness* | VEALL, Archibald | *Barrister* |
| SMITH, Francis | *HMS Stephen Furness* | VOS, H C | *Barrister* |
| SMITH, John | *HMT Waltham* | WAKEFORD, Charles | *HMS Champagne* |
| SMITH, William Edward | *HMS Cullist* | WALLIS, John Edwin | *HMS Stephen Furness* |
| SOREL-CAMERON, Herbert Augustus | *HMS Stephen Furness* | WALMSLEY, Silas | *G A Savage* |
| | | WALTER, Eric Douglas | *HMS Champagne* |
| SOUTHALL, Sidney | *HMS Stephen Furness* | WALTER, Hubert Norman | *HMS Cullist* |
| SOUTHWELL, Alfred | *HMS Stephen Furness* | WARD, Oliver | *HMS Champagne* |
| STACK, John | *Dundalk* | WATERSON, William Benjamin | *HMS Champagne* |
| STANNARD, Charles Edward | *HMS Champagne* | | |
| STEBBINGS, Henry Edwin | *HMS Cullist* | WATKINS, Joseph | *HMS Champagne* |
| STEEL, John Edmund | *PT1* | WATT, R D | *HMS Stephen Furness* |
| STEPHEN, Peter Strachan | *HMT Waltham* | WATTERSON, William Henry | *G A Savage* |
| STEVENS, George Philip Lancelot | *HMS Stephen Furness* | WEBSTER, William John | *HMT Waltham* |
| | | WENBORNE, William | *HMS Stephen Furness* |
| STEVENS, Sidney James | *HMS Stephen Furness* | WEST, William E | *HMS Champagne* |
| STEWART, James White | *HMT Waltham* | WHITCHURCH, Frederick Thomas | *HMS Cullist* |
| STOCK, Albert | *HMS Champagne* | | |
| STONE, Ernest William | *HMS Stephen Furness* | WHITE, George Harold Edward | *HMS Cullist* |
| STOTT, James | *HMS Champagne* | | |
| STOWELL, Daniel | *Dundalk* | WHITE, William | *Romeo* |
| STRACHAN, Robert | *HMT Waltham* | WHITE, William John | *HMS Stephen Furness* |
| SUCCAMORE, William J | *HMS Champagne* | WHITTON, David John | *HMS Cullist* |
| SULLIVAN, D | *Kenmare* | WHITWAM, Arthur Edward | *HMS Champagne* |
| SWANGER, T S | *PT1* | WIGMORE, A E | *HMS Stephen Furness* |
| SWEETMAN, Peter | *HMS Champagne* | WILKINSON, Harold | *Leinster* |
| | | WILLIAMS, Bertram Percy | *Romeo* |
| | | WILLIAMS, David | *G A Savage* |

| NAME | VESSEL |
|---|---|
| WILLIAMS, Frank David | *HMS Stephen Furness* |
| WILLIAMSON, Edward Thomas | *HMS Stephen Furness* |
| WILSON, David | *HMT Waltham* |
| WINGATE, John William | *HMS Stephen Furness* |
| WINSLOW, Thomas Maitland | *HMS Stephen Furness* |
| WOODALL, Ernest | *HMS Cullist* |
| WOODHOUSE, James | *HMS Stephen Furness* |
| WYBROW, Thomas James | *HMS Stephen Furness* |
| YOUNG, Alfred | *Calista* |
| YOUNG, Charles | *PT1* |
| YOUNG, Richard | *Barrister* |

# Index of known survivors

| NAME | VESSEL | NAME | VESSEL |
|---|---|---|---|
| ARTHUR, John | *Inkosi* | CORTEEN, H | *Ben Rein* |
| BANNON, W | *Liverpool* | COWLEY, John | *Ben Rein* |
| BARRY, James | *Kenmare* | COWLEY, J W | *Ben Rein* |
| BINGHAM | *HMS Champagne* | COX, W J | *HMS Champagne* |
| BOYD, T | *Liverpool* | CUBBIN, John | *Princess Victoria* |
| BRIDSON, J | *Ben Rein* | CUTHBERTSON, James | *Barrister* |
| BROUGHAM, Joseph | *Kenmare* | DAUGHERTY, Harold | *Marguerite* |
| BROWN, J | *PT1* | DEERY, Francis | *Dundalk* |
| BROWN, Percy G | *HMS Champagne* | DEVANEY, John Francis | *Liverpool* |
| BURNS, J | *Liverpool* | ELLIS, John | *Linda Blanche* |
| BYRNE, Patrick | *Dundalk* | ERICKSON, James | *Downshire* |
| CAMOMILE, William | *Romeo* | EVANS, E | *PT1* |
| CARDSWELL, James | *Downshire* | EVANS, William | *Kenmare* |
| CARLYLE, Thomas | *Downshire* | FERGUSON, Angus | *Dundalk* |
| CARRAN, H J | *Ben Rein* | FIFE | *PT1* |
| CASPER, C | *PT1* | FITZGERALD, Thomas | *Dundalk* |
| CHALK, Frederick | *HMS Stephen Furness* | FRANCIS, Joseph Thomas | *Carmelite* |
| CHRISTIAN, William | *HMS Champagne* | FRENCH, Lawrence Joseph | *Barrister* |
| CHRISTIDIS, L | *Mikelis* | FRENGOPOULOS, Gerasimis | *Mikelis* |
| CLARK, R S | *HMS Stephen Furness* | FRENGOPOULOS, Gerasimos | *Mikelis* |
| CLUTTERBUCK, Ernest | *Conargo* | FRENGOPOULOS, Spiros | *Mikelis* |
| COLVIN, J | *Princess Victoria* | GALBRAITH, William | *Limesfield* |
| COMPAGNON, John | *Romeo* | GORRY, C | *Princess Victoria* |
| CON | *HMS Champagne* | GOULANDRIS, A | *Mikelis* |
| CONNOR, John | *Downshire* | GREER, William | *HMS Stephen Furness* |
| CONNOR, William Henry | *Downshire* | GREGOS, P | *Mikelis* |
| CORLETT, T | *Ben Rein* | GRIFFITHS, W N | *Inkosi* |

| NAME | VESSEL | NAME | VESSEL |
|---|---|---|---|
| HARRIS, George | *HMS Stephen Furness* | MORRISON, Alex | *Downshire* |
| HEGGIE | *Ben Cruachan* | MORRISON, W | *Princess Victoria* |
| HIGGINS, John | *Dundalk* | MULLAN, John | *Downshire* |
| HOCKRIDGE | *PT1* | MULQUEEN, John | *Dundalk* |
| HORSBURGH, William | *Largo* | MURPHY, Henry | *Downshire* |
| HUDSON, T | *Princess Victoria* | NALDER | *HMS Champagne* |
| ISOURIS, M | *Mikelis* | NERATYIS, E | *Mikelis* |
| JOHANNSSAN, Hans | *Sarpfos* | NOONAN, P | *Dundalk* |
| KATHARIS, L | *Mikelis* | O'BRIEN, Tim | *Kenmare* |
| KEARNEY, Patrick | *Dundalk* | O'CONNOR, Timothy | *Dundalk* |
| KEENAN, James | *HMS Champagne* | O'DONNELL | *PT1* |
| KERR, M D | *PT1* | OLIVIERO, M | *Mikelis* |
| KILGALLEN, J | *Liverpool* | OLSSON, John | *HMS Stephen Furness* |
| KILLEY, Ed | *Princess Victoria* | O'NEILL, Hugh | *Dundalk* |
| KILLEY, N | *Princess Victoria* | PAGE, John | *Dalewood* |
| KINLEY, Hugh C | *Princess Victoria* | PETRATOS, S | *Mikelis* |
| KINLEY, James | *HMS Champagne* | PETRIE, A | *Liverpool* |
| KOUTOS, T | *Mikelis* | PETROPOULOS, E | *Mikelis* |
| KRAUKLE, John | *Nadejda* | PHILLIPS, Arthur | *Kenmare* |
| KRISTIS, M | *Mikelis* | PRAGNELL, Herbert Clifton | *HMS Stephen Furness* |
| LEE, Richard | *Marguerite* | PRODOMAS, E | *Mikelis* |
| LEE, Thomas | *Marguerite* | QUIRK, Evan | *Bessy* |
| LEISKARIS, N | *Mikelis* | RIPPIN, W E | *Barrister* |
| LEWIN, J | *Ben Rein* | SADDINGTON, Charles | *HMS Stephen Furness* |
| LOULYOS, A | *Mikelis* | SCOLIDIS, D | *Mikelis* |
| LUCAS, J | *PT1* | SEDDON, A H | *PT1* |
| LYNGNANE, James Arthur | *HMS Stephen Furness* | SEDDON, Arthur | *Romeo* |
| McAVOY, Lawrence | *HMS Stephen Furness* | SHERINGHAM, H W | *HMS Stephen Furness* |
| McCOFFEY, William Hugh | *Ardbeg* | SIMMONDS, P S | *HMS Stephen Furness* |
| McCOURT, Patrick | *Dundalk* | SIMPSON, S H | *HMS Cullist* |
| McDONALD, J | *PT1* | SIRIGOS, M | *Mikelis* |
| McGOWAN, J | *Liverpool* | SLINGER, William | *Sunrise* |
| McGOWAN, James | *Liverpool* | SMARAGILIS, G | *Mikelis* |
| McGOWAN, William | *Downshire* | SMITH, J | *Liverpool* |
| McLOUGLIN, Michael | *Liverpool* | SMITH, J | *Liverpool* |
| MAHUGH, S A | *Inkosi* | TEASDALE, J | *PT1* |
| MARTIN, William | *Downshire* | THOMAS, Ivor | *Liverpool* |
| MAVROGIANIS, D | *Mikelis* | TUITE, James | *Dundalk* |
| MENEELY, James | *Kilcoan* | TURNBULL, Thomas | *Downshire* |
| MILES, Charles | *Wave* | WARE, W J | *HMS Champagne* |
| MILLS, James | *Conargo* | WINFIELD, J C | *HMS Stephen Furness* |
| MOFFATT, J | *Liverpool* | WOOD, Harold | *Barrister* |
| MOFFATT, John | *Liverpool* | WOODS, G | *PT1* |
| MOORE, Frank | *HMS Champagne* | WRIGHT, James | *Kenmare* |
| | | ZAFIRAKY, D | *Mikelis* |

# U-Boats involved – details, history and fates

Deck guns were changed on U-Boats during the war so the final armament configuration is given here.

## *U-19*

| | |
|---|---|
| Type | U 19 |
| Shipyard | Kaiserliche Werft, Danzig (Yard number 13) |
| Tonnage | 837 tonnes displacement (submerged), 650 tonnes displacement (surfaced) |
| Dimensions | 64.2 m x 6.1 m x 3.6 m |
| Engines | 2 x 8-cylinder 2-stroke diesel engines by MAN – 1,700 hp |
| | 2 x electric motors by AEG – 1,200 hp |
| Surface Speed | 15.4 knots |
| Submerged Speed | 9.5 knots |
| Range | 7,600 nautical miles (surfaced), 80 nautical miles (submerged) |
| Complement | 35 men |
| Armament | 6 torpedoes, 2 bow tubes, 2 stern tubes |
| | 105 mm deck gun (200 rounds) |
| Commissioned | 6th July 1913 |
| Career | 12 patrols: 1st August 1914 to 19th September 1916 – III Flotilla; 19th September 1916 to 1st May 1917 – Baltic Flotilla; 1st May 1917 to 11th November 1918 – III Flotilla |
| Successes | 57 ships sunk – 97,893 tons, 1 warship sunk – 1,261 tons, 3 ships damaged – 4,224 tons, 1 ship taken as prize – 733 tons |
| Fate | 24th November 1918 – Surrendered. Broken up at Blyth in 1919/20. |

# U-20

| | |
|---|---|
| Type | U 19 |
| Shipyard | Kaiserliche Werft, Danzig (Yard number 14) |
| Tonnage | 837 tonnes displacement (submerged), 650 tonnes displacement (surfaced) |
| Dimensions | 64.2 m x 6.1 m x 3.6 m |
| Engines | 2 x 8-cylinder 2-stroke diesel engines by MAN – 1,700 hp |
| | 2 x electric motors by AEG – 1,200 hp |
| Surface Speed | 15.4 knots |
| Submerged Speed | 9.5 knots |
| Range | 7,600 nautical miles (surfaced), 80 nautical miles (submerged) |
| Complement | 35 men |
| Armament | 6 torpedoes, 2 bow tubes, 2 stern tubes |
| | 2 x 88 mm deck guns (300 rounds) |
| Commissioned | 5th August 1913 |
| Career | 7 patrols: 1st August 1914 to 4th November 1916 – III Flotilla |
| Successes | 37 ships sunk – 145,830 tons, 2 ships damaged – 2,643 tons |
| Fate | 4th November 1916 – Grounded on the Danish coast near Vrist and blown up by her crew the next day. Wreck blown up on 26th August 1925. |

# U-21

| | |
|---|---|
| Type | U 19 |
| Shipyard | Kaiserliche Werft, Danzig (Yard number 15) |
| Tonnage | 837 tonnes displacement (submerged), 650 tonnes displacement (surfaced) |
| Dimensions | 64.2 m x 6.1 m x 3.6 m |
| Engines | 2 x 8-cylinder 2-stroke diesel engines by MAN – 1,700 hp |
| | 2 x electric motors by AEG – 1,200 hp |
| Surface Speed | 15.4 knots |
| Submerged Speed | 9.5 knots |
| Range | 7,600 nautical miles (surfaced), 80 miles (submerged) |
| Complement | 35 men |
| Armament | 6 torpedoes, 2 bow tubes, 2 stern tubes |
| | 2 x 88 mm deck guns (300 rounds) |
| Commissioned | 22nd October 1913 |
| Career | 11 patrols: 1st August 1914 to 5th June 1915 – III Flotilla; 5th June 1915 to unknown date – Constantinople Flotilla; date unknown to 4th March 1917 – Pola Flotilla; 4th March 1917 to 11th November 1918 – III Flotilla |
| Successes | 36 ships sunk – 79,005 tons, 2 ships damaged – 8,918 tons, 4 warships sunk – 34,575 tons |
| Fate | 22nd February 1919 – Sank in the North Sea while under tow by a British warship. |

# U-27

| | |
|---|---|
| Type | U 27 |
| Shipyard | Kaiserliche Werft, Danzig (Yard number 17) |
| Tonnage | 867 tonnes displacement (submerged), 675 tonnes displacement (surfaced) |
| Dimensions | 64.7 m x 6.3 m x 3.5 m |
| Engines | 2 x 6-cylinder 4-stroke diesel engines by MAN – 2,000 hp |
| | 2 x electric motors by AEG – 1,200 hp |
| Surface Speed | 16.7 knots |
| Submerged Speed | 9.8 knots |
| Range | 9,770 nautical miles (surfaced), 85 nautical miles (submerged) |
| Complement | 37 men |
| Armament | 6 torpedoes, 2 bow tubes, 2 stern tubes |
| | 2 x 88 mm deck guns (300 rounds) |
| Commissioned | 8th May 1914 |
| Career | 3 patrols: 1st August 1914 to 19th August 1915 – IV Flotilla |
| Successes | 10 ships sunk – 31,120 tons, 2 warships sunk – 6,325 tons |
| Fate | 19th August 1915 – Sunk by gunfire from the Q-ship *Barralong* in the Western Approaches. All 37 hands lost. |

# U-30

| | |
|---|---|
| Type | U 27 |
| Shipyard | Kaiserliche Werft, Danzig (Yard number 20) |
| Tonnage | 867 tonnes displacement (submerged), 791 tonnes displacement (surfaced) |
| Dimensions | 64.7 m x 6.3 m x 3.5 m |
| Engines | 2 x 6-cylinder 4-stroke diesel engines by MAN – 2,000 hp |
| | 2 x electric motors by AEG – 1,200 hp |
| Surface Speed | 16.7 knots |
| Submerged Speed | 9.8 knots |
| Range | 9,770 nautical miles (surfaced), 85 nautical miles (submerged) |
| Complement | 35 men |
| Armament | 6 torpedoes, 2 bow tubes, 2 stern tubes |
| | 105 mm deck gun (200 rounds) |
| Commissioned | 26th August 1914 |
| Career | 6 patrols: date unknown to 22nd June 1915 – IV Flotilla; 15th October 1916 to 19th November 1917 – IV Flotilla; 19th November 1917 to 11th November 1918 – Training Flotilla |
| Successes | 27 ships sunk – 48,060 tons, 1 ship damaged – 5,189 tons |
| Fate | 22nd November 1918 – Surrendered. Broken up at Blyth in 1919/20. |

# U-69

| | |
|---|---|
| Type | U 66 |
| Shipyard | Germaniawerft, Kiel (Yard number 206) |
| Tonnage | 933 tonnes displacement (submerged), 791 tonnes displacement (surfaced) |
| Dimensions | 69.5 m x 6.3 m x 3.8 m |
| Engines | 2 x 6-cylinder 4-cycle diesel engines by Germania – 2,300 hp |
| | 2 x electric motors by Pichler & Co – 1,240 hp |
| Surface Speed | 16.8 knots |
| Submerged Speed | 10.3 knots |
| Range | 7,370 nautical miles (surfaced), 115 nautical miles (submerged) |
| Complement | 40 men |
| Armament | 12 torpedoes, 4 bow tubes, 1 stern tube |
| | 105 mm deck gun (120 rounds) |
| Commissioned | 4th September 1915 |
| Career | 6 patrols: 4th March 1916 to 23rd July 1917 – IV Flotilla |
| Successes | 31 ships sunk – 102,875 tons, 1 ship damaged – 1,648 tons |
| Fate | Last contact on 11th July 1917 while en route to patrol off Ireland. U-69 may have sunk the steamship *Mikelis* on 24th July 1917 off Peel but there are doubts over this attribution. She may also have been responsible for the attack on *HMS Berwick* off the Calf of Man on 25th July 1917. Listed as missing in the Irish Sea after 24th July 1917 with the loss of all 40 hands. |

# U-80

| | |
|---|---|
| Type | UE 1 |
| Shipyard | AG Vulcan, Hamburg (Yard number 62) |
| Tonnage | 832 tonnes displacement (submerged), 755 tonnes displacement (surfaced) |
| Dimensions | 56.8 m x 5.9 m x 4.9 m |
| Engines | 2 x 6-cylinder 2-stroke diesel engines by Körting – 900 hp |
| | 2 x electric motors by SSW – 900 hp |
| Surface Speed | 9.9 knots |
| Submerged Speed | 7.9 knots |
| Range | 7,880 nautical miles (surfaced), 83 nautical miles (submerged) |
| Complement | 32 men |
| Armament | 4 torpedoes, 1 bow tube, 1 stern tube |
| | 105 mm deck gun (130 rounds) |
| | 2 x 100 cm mine launching tubes at the stern |
| | 38 x UE 150 mines |
| Commissioned | 6th June 1916 |
| Career | 17 patrols: 27th August 1916 to 11th November 1918 – I Flotilla |
| Successes | 25 ships sunk – 48,880 tons, 1 warship sunk – 1,025 tons; 4 ships damaged – 35,608 tons |
| Fate | 16th January 1919 – Surrendered. Broken up at Swansea in 1922. |

# U-86

| | |
|---|---|
| Type | U 81 |
| Shipyard | Germaniawerft, Kiel (Yard number 256) |
| Tonnage | 946 tonnes displacement (submerged), 808 tonnes displacement (surfaced) |
| Dimensions | 70.0 m x 6.3 m x 4.0 m |
| Engines | 2 x 6-cylinder 4-stroke diesel engines by MAN – 2,400 hp |
| | 2 x electric motors by SSW – 1,200 hp |
| Surface Speed | 16.8 knots |
| Submerged Speed | 9.1 knots |
| Range | 11,220 nautical miles (surfaced), 56 nautical miles (submerged) |
| Complement | 35 men |
| Armament | 12 torpedoes, 4 bow tubes, 2 stern tubes |
| | 105 mm deck gun (140 rounds) |
| | 88 mm deck gun (220 rounds) |
| Commissioned | 30th November 1916 |
| Career | 12 patrols: 21st February 1917 to 11th November 1918 – IV Flotilla |
| Successes | 33 ships sunk – 117,583 tons, 1 ship damaged – 163 tons |
| Fate | 20th November 1918 – Surrendered. Sank in the English Channel on the way to be broken up in 1921. |

# U-90

| | |
|---|---|
| Type | U 87 |
| Shipyard | Kaiserliche Werft, Danzig (Yard number 34) |
| Tonnage | 998 tonnes displacement (submerged), 757 tonnes displacement (surfaced) |
| Dimensions | 65.8 m x 6.2 m x 3.9 m |
| Engines | 2 x 6-cylinder 4-stroke diesel engines by MAN – 2,400 hp |
| | 2 x electric motors by SSW – 1,200 hp |
| Surface Speed | 15.6 knots |
| Submerged Speed | 8.6 knots |
| Range | 11,380 nautical miles (surfaced), 56 nautical miles (submerged) |
| Complement | 36 men |
| Armament | 12 torpedoes, 2 bow tubes, 2 stern tubes |
| | 105 mm deck gun (140 rounds) |
| | 88 mm deck gun (220 rounds) |
| Commissioned | 2nd August 1917 |
| Career | 7 patrols: 10th September 1917 to 11th November 1918 – III Flotilla |
| Successes | 30 ships sunk – 74,175 tons, 2 ships damaged – 8,594 tons |
| Fate | 20th November 1918 – Surrendered. Broken up at Bo'ness in 1919. |

# U-91

| | |
|---|---|
| Type | U 87 |
| Shipyard | Kaiserliche Werft, Danzig (Yard number 35) |
| Tonnage | 998 tonnes displacement (submerged), 757 tonnes displacement (surfaced) |
| Dimensions | 65.8 m x 6.2 m x 3.9 m |
| Engines | 2 x 6-cylinder 4-stroke diesel engines by MAN – 2,400 hp |
| | 2 x electric motors by SSW – 1,200 hp |
| Surface Speed | 15.6 knots |
| Submerged Speed | 8.6 knots |
| Range | 11,380 nautical miles (surfaced), 56 nautical miles (submerged) |
| Complement | 36 men |
| Armament | 12 torpedoes, 2 bow tubes, 2 stern tubes |
| | 105 mm deck gun (140 rounds) |
| | 88 mm deck gun (220 rounds) |
| Commissioned | 17th September 1917 |
| Career | 8 patrols: 13th December 1917 to 11th November 1918 – III Flotilla |
| Successes | 37 ships sunk – 87,119 tons, 2 ships damaged – 11,821 tons |
| Fate | 26th November 1918 – Surrendered to France. Broken up at Brest in July 1921. |

# U-96

| | |
|---|---|
| Type | U 93 |
| Shipyard | Germaniawerft, Kiel (Yard number 260) |
| Tonnage 9 | 98 tonnes displacement (submerged), 837 tonnes displacement (surfaced) |
| Dimensions | 71.6 m x 6.3 m x 3.9 m |
| Engines | 2 x 6-cylinder 2-stroke diesel engines by Germania – 2,300 hp |
| | 2 x electric motors by SSW – 1,200 hp |
| Surface Speed | 16.9 knots |
| Submerged Speed | 8.6 knots |
| Range | 8,290 nautical miles (surfaced), 47 nautical miles (submerged) |
| Complement | 39 men |
| Armament | 16 torpedoes, 4 bow tubes, 2 stern tubes |
| | 105 mm deck gun (140 rounds) |
| | 88 mm deck gun (220 rounds) |
| Commissioned | 11th April 1917 |
| Career | 9 patrols: 24th May 1917 to 11th November 1918 – IV Flotilla |
| Successes | 31 ships sunk – 95,253 tons, 3 ships damaged – 16,220 tons |
| Fate | 20th November 1918 – Surrendered. Broken up at Bo'ness in 1919/20. |

# U-97

| | |
|---|---|
| Type | U 93 |
| Shipyard | Germaniawerft, Kiel (Yard number 261) |
| Tonnage | 998 tonnes displacement (submerged), 837 tonnes displacement (surfaced) |
| Dimensions | 71.6 m x 6.3 m x 3.9 m |
| Engines | 2 x 6-cylinder 2-stroke diesel engines by Germania – 2,300 hp |
| | 2 x electric motors by SSW – 1,200 hp |
| Surface Speed | 16.9 knots |
| Submerged Speed | 8.6 knots |
| Range | 8,290 nautical miles (surfaced), 47 nautical miles (submerged) |
| Complement | 39 men |
| Armament | 16 torpedoes, 4 bow tubes, 2 stern tubes |
| | 105 mm deck gun (140 rounds) |
| Commissioned | 16th May 1917 |
| Career | 5 patrols: 27th August 1917 to 11th November 1918 – IV Flotilla |
| Successes | 4 ships sunk – 2,089 tons, 1 ship damaged – 4,785 tons |
| Fate | 21st November 1918 – Sank in the North Sea on passage to surrender. |

# U-102

| | |
|---|---|
| Type | U 57 |
| Shipyard | AG Weser, Bremen (Yard number 253) |
| Tonnage | 952 tonnes displacement (submerged), 750 tonnes displacement (surfaced) |
| Dimensions | 67.6 m x 6.3 m x 3.7 m |
| Engines | 2 x 6-cylinder 4-stroke diesel engines by MAN – 2,400 hp |
| | 2 x electric motors by SSW – 1,200 hp |
| Surface Speed | 16.5 knots |
| Submerged Speed | 8.8 knots |
| Range | 10,100 nautical miles (surfaced), 45 nautical miles (submerged) |
| Complement | 42 men |
| Armament | 12 torpedoes, 2 bow tubes, 2 stern tubes |
| | 105 mm deck gun (205 rounds) |
| | 88 mm deck gun (220 rounds) |
| Commissioned | 18th June 1917 |
| Career | 7 patrols: 5th August 1917 to 30th September 1918 – II Flotilla |
| Successes | 4 ships sunk – 9,140 tons, 1 ship damaged – 10,757 tons |
| Fate | 30th September 1918 – Mined in the Northern Barrage east of the Orkney Islands while homeward bound about 28th to 30th September 1918. All 42 hands lost. |

# U-104

| | |
|---|---|
| Type | U 57 |
| Shipyard | AG Weser, Bremen (Yard number 255) |
| Tonnage | 952 tonnes displacement (submerged), 750 tonnes displacement (surfaced) |
| Dimensions | 67.6 m x 6.3 m x 3.7 m |
| Engines | 2 x 6-cylinder 4-stroke diesel engines by MAN – 2,400 hp |
| | 2 x electric motors by SSW – 1,200 hp |
| Surface Speed | 16.5 knots |
| Submerged Speed | 8.8 knots |
| Range | 10,100 nautical miles (surfaced), 45 nautical miles (submerged) |
| Complement | 42 men |
| Armament | 12 torpedoes, 2 bow tubes, 2 stern tubes |
| | 105 mm deck gun (205 rounds) |
| | 88 mm deck gun (220 rounds) |
| Commissioned | 12th August 1917 |
| Career | 4 patrols: 1st October 1917 to 25th April 1918 – II Flotilla |
| Successes | 8 ships sunk – 10,795 tons |
| Fate | 25th April 1918 – Depth charged and sunk by *HMS Jessamine* in St George's Channel. 41 hands lost and 1 survivor. |

# U-105

| | |
|---|---|
| Type | U 93 |
| Shipyard | Germaniawerft, Kiel (Yard number 274) |
| Tonnage | 1,000 tonnes displacement (submerged), 798 tonnes displacement (surfaced) |
| Dimensions | 71.6 m x 6.3 m x 3.9 m |
| Engines | 2 x 6-cylinder 4-stroke diesel engines by MAN – 2,400 hp |
| | 2 x electric motors by SSW – 1,200 hp |
| Surface Speed | 16.4 knots |
| Submerged Speed | 8.4 knots |
| Range | 9,280 nautical miles (surfaced), 50 nautical miles (submerged) |
| Complement | 36 men |
| Armament | 16 torpedoes, 4 bow tubes, 2 stern tubes |
| | 105 mm deck gun (140 rounds) |
| | 88 mm deck gun (220 rounds) |
| Commissioned | 4th July 1917 |
| Career | 6 patrols: 3rd September 1917 to 11th November 1918 – IV Flotilla |
| Successes | 19 ships sunk – 55,834 tons, 2 ships damaged |
| Fate | 20th November 1918 – surrendered to France. Became the French submarine *Jean Autric* and eventually was broken up in 1938. |

# UB-57

| | |
|---|---|
| Type | UB III |
| Shipyard | AG Weser, Bremen (Yard number 269) |
| Tonnage | 646 tonnes displacement (submerged), 516 tonnes displacement (surfaced) |
| Dimensions | 55.9 m x 5.8 m x 3.7 m |
| Engines | 2 x 6-cylinder 4-stroke diesel engines by Körting – 1,060 hp |
| | 2 x electric motors by SSW – 788 hp |
| Surface Speed | 13.4 knots |
| Submerged Speed | 7.8 knots |
| Range | 9,020 nautical miles (surfaced), 55 nautical miles (submerged) |
| Complement | 34 men |
| Armament | 10 torpedoes, 4 bow tubes, 1 stern tube |
| | 88 mm deck gun (160 rounds) |
| Commissioned | 30th July 1917 |
| Career | 11 patrols: 20th September 1917 to 14th August 1918 – Flandern I Flotilla |
| Successes | 47 ships sunk – 129,173 tons, 10 ships damaged – 58,990 tons |
| Fate | 14th August 1918 – Mined off the Flanders coast. All 34 hands lost. |

# UB-64

| | |
|---|---|
| Type | UB III |
| Shipyard | AG Vulcan, Hamburg (Yard number 89) |
| Tonnage | 639 tonnes displacement (submerged), 508 tonnes displacement (surfaced) |
| Dimensions | 55.3 m x 5.8 m x 3.7 m |
| Engines | 2 x 6-cylinder 4-stroke diesel engines by MAN – 1,100 hp |
| | 2 x electric motors by SSW – 788 hp |
| Surface Speed | 13.3 knots |
| Submerged Speed | 8.0 knots |
| Range | 8,420 nautical miles (surfaced), 55 nautical miles (submerged) |
| Complement | 34 men |
| Armament | 10 torpedoes, 4 bow tubes, 1 stern tube |
| | 105 mm deck gun (108 rounds) |
| Commissioned | 5th August 1917 |
| Career | 8 patrols: 10th September 1917 to 20th April 1918 – V Flotilla; 20th April 1918 to 11th November 1918 – II Flotilla |
| Successes | 29 ships sunk – 33,740 tons, 4 ships damaged – 48,497 tons, 1 ship taken as a prize – 371 tons |
| Fate | 21st November 1918 – Surrendered. Broken up at Fareham in 1921. |

# UB-77

| | |
|---|---|
| Type | UB III |
| Shipyard | Blohm and Voss, Hamburg (Yard number 306) |
| Tonnage | 648 tonnes displacement (submerged), 516 tonnes displacement (surfaced) |
| Dimensions | 55.3 m x 5.8 m x 3.7 m |
| Engines | 2 x 6-cylinder 4-stroke diesel engines by MAN – 1,100 hp |
| | 2 x electric motors by SSW – 788 hp |
| Surface Speed | 13.6 knots |
| Submerged Speed | 7.8 knots |
| Range | 8,680 nautical miles (surfaced), 55 nautical miles (submerged) |
| Complement | 34 men |
| Armament | 10 torpedoes, 4 bow tubes, 1 stern tube |
| | 105 mm deck gun (108 rounds) |
| Commissioned | 2nd October 1917 |
| Career | 7 patrols: 30th November 1917 to 17th April 1918 – V Flotilla; 17th April 1918 to 11th November 1918 – I Flotilla |
| Successes | 1 ship sunk – 14,348 tons, 2 ships damaged – 28,174 tons |
| Fate | 16th January 1919 – Surrendered. Broken up at Swansea in 1922. |

# UB-123

| | |
|---|---|
| Type | UB III |
| Shipyard | AG Weser, Bremen (Yard number 296) |
| Tonnage | 643 tonnes displacement (submerged), 512 tonnes displacement (surfaced) |
| Dimensions | 55.9 m x 5.8 m x 3.7 m |
| Engines | 2 x 6-cylinder 4-stroke diesel engines by Körting – 1,060 hp |
| | 2 x electric motors by SSW – 788 hp |
| Surface Speed | 13.9 knots |
| Submerged Speed | 7.6 knots |
| Range | 7,280 nautical miles (surfaced), 55 nautical miles (submerged) |
| Complement | 36 men |
| Armament | 10 torpedoes, 4 bow tubes, 1 stern tube |
| | 88 mm deck gun (160 rounds) |
| Commissioned | 6th April 1918 |
| Career | 2 patrols: 22nd June 1918 to 19th October 1918 – III Flotilla |
| Successes | 1 ship sunk –2,646 tons, 3 ships taken as prizes – 3,530 tons |
| Fate | 19th October 1918 – Most likely mined in the Northern Barrage. All 36 hands lost. |

# UC-75

| | |
|---|---|
| Type | UC II |
| Shipyard | AG Vulcan, Hamburg (Yard number 80) |
| Tonnage | 493 tons displacement (submerged), 410 tonnes displacement (surfaced) |
| Dimensions | 50.5 m x 5.2 m x 3.7 m |
| Engines | 2 x 6-cylinder 4-stroke diesel engines by Körting – 600 hp |
| | 2 x electric motors by SSW – 580 hp |
| Surface Speed | 11.8 knots |
| Submerged Speed | 7.3 knots |
| Range | 10,230 nautical miles (surfaced), 52 nautical miles (submerged) |
| Complement | 26 men |
| Armament | 7 torpedoes, 2 bow tubes, 1 stern tube |
| | 88 mm deck gun (133 rounds) |
| | 6 x 100 cm mine launching tubes |
| | 18 x type UC200 mines |
| Commissioned | 6th December 1916 |
| Career | 13 patrols: 10th February 1917 to 5th August 1917 – I Flotilla; 5th August 1917 to 31st May 1918 – Flandern/Flandern II Flotilla |
| Successes | 56 ships sunk – 80,509 tons, 8 ships damaged – 40,021 tons; 2 warships sunk – 1,555 tons |
| Fate | 31st May 1918 – Rammed and sunk by *HMS Fairy* while attacking a convoy in the North Sea. 19 hands lost (unknown number of survivors). |

Technical details on U-Boats vary depending on the source of information used. The details quoted in this section are derived from the book *"German Warships 1815-1945 Volume Two – U-Boats and Mine Warfare Vessels"* by Erich Gröner, which is acknowledged as one of the leading sources of U-Boat technical and historical data.

# Glossary of unusual terms used in the book

| | |
|---|---|
| **Awthartship** | Across the ship from side to side |
| **Gun layer** | The person who controls the angle of elevation of a gun. |
| **HMD** | His Majesty's Drifter |
| **HMS** | His Majesty's Ship |
| **HMT** | His Majesty's Trawler |
| **Lyddite Shell** | First British high explosive shell introduced in 1896. |
| **'Magnetic'** | Bearing from a known geographical point using a compass (the declination from true north in World War One was about 17 degrees to the west). |
| **MMR** | Mercantile Marine Reserve |
| **Quarter** | The upper portion of the after side of a ship, usually between the aftermost mast and the stern. |
| **RMLI** | Royal Marine Light Infantry |
| **RMS** | Royal Mail Steamer |
| **RNCVR** | Royal Navy Canadian Volunteer Reserve |
| **RNR** | Royal Navy Reserve |
| **RNVR** | Royal Navy Volunteer Reserve |
| **ST** | Steam trawler |
| **'True'** | Bearing from a known geographical point using a chart and the true North Pole. |
| **Zigzagging** | Zigzagging (randomly changing course) was used in ships to keep any tracking submarine from gaining a viable target solution, which is vital information required for the torpedo settings prior to shooting. It takes time to calculate specific targeting solution information, and if the ship changes course often enough it makes it extremely difficult for the submarine's tracking party to effectively gain a proper solution for firing. |

# Sources of information

The following were used as general sources of information. Paper and internet sources for each specific event are given at the end of the event.

Brady K., McKeon C., Lyttleton J., & Lawler I. 2012. Warships, U-Boats & Liners, A Guide to Shipwrecks Mapped in Irish Waters. Government of Ireland. Dublin.

Gibson R.H. & Prendergast M. 2002. The German Submarine War 1914-1918. Periscope Publishing Ltd. Penzance.

Gray E.A. 1994. The U-Boat War 1914-1918. LEO COOPER. London.

Gröner, E. 1991. German Warships 1815-1945 Volume Two U-Boats and Mine Warfare Vessels. Conway Maritime Press Limited. London.

Koerver, H.J. 2010. German Submarine Warfare 1914-1918 in the Eyes of British Intelligence. LIS Reinisch. Steinbach.

Stokes R. 2004. U-Boat Alley, The U-Boat War in the Irish Channel During World War 1. Compuwreck. Gorey, County Wexford.

# Index